SCOPE—Spoken Communication: An Open-plan Project in Education

General Editor: Christabel Burniston, The English Speaking Board
Executive Editor: Esmor Jones
Publisher: Robert Maxwell, M.C., M.P.

CREATIVE ORAL ASSESSMENT

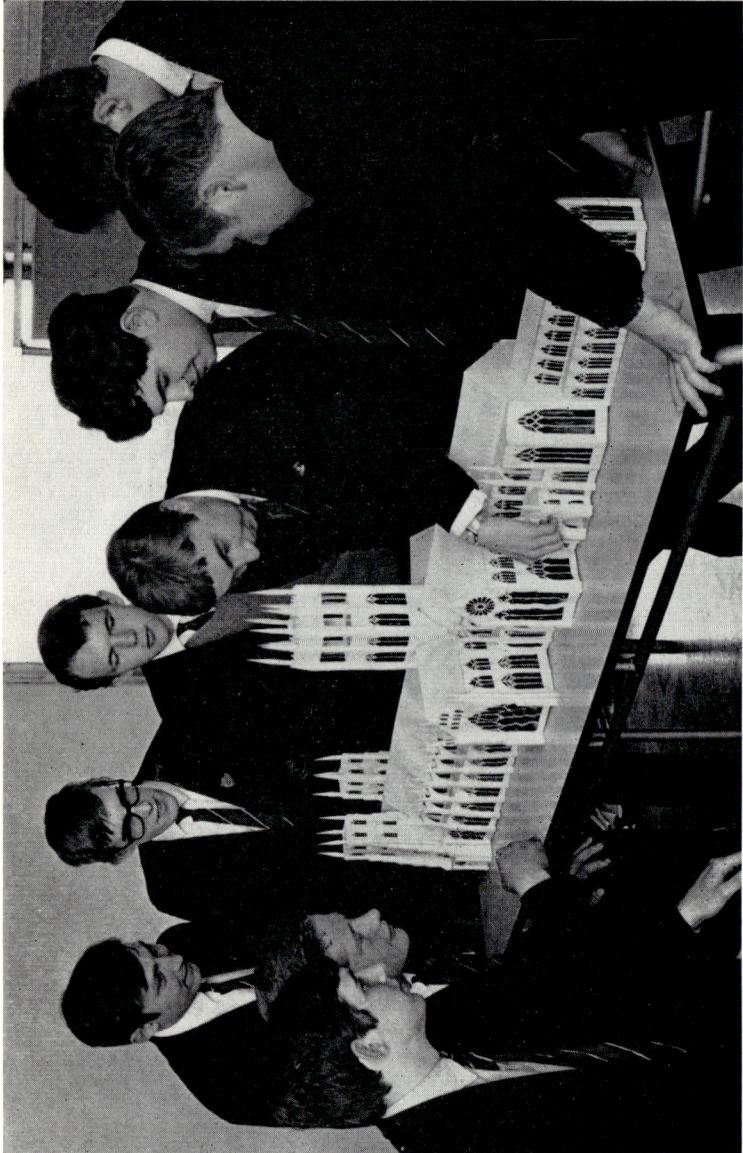

CREATIVE ORAL ASSESSMENT

Its Scope and Stimulus

BY

CHRISTABEL BURNISTON

THE QUEEN'S AWARD
TO INDUSTRY 1968

PERGAMON PRESS

PERGAMON PRESS LTD.
OXFORD · LONDON · EDINBURGH
NEW YORK · TORONTO · SYDNEY

First Edition 1968   Copyright © 1968
CHRISTABEL BURNISTON
Library of Congress Catalog Card No. 68–18892

Printed by T. Nelson (Printers) Ltd, London and Edinburgh

08 003767 4

Contents

Foreword

THE model cathedral in the photograph is the work of Philip, seen here leaning over and explaining the structure of the doorway to some of his fellow sixth-formers at Smithells Technical High School, Bolton. The occasion was an English Speaking Board examination, and the photograph itself was taken by another boy, Lewis, whose personal project was Interior Photography.

Presenting his Personal Project, Philip revealed that this was one of several models he had made over the years, as a Christmas decoration for a mental hospital: "Their only outing is to church, so I thought this would mean something to them."

When the examiner invited Philip's friends to question him, he explained that the model was of a cathedral of his imagination, a composite of inspirations from Lichfield, Canterbury and York.

Genuine enquiry produced a great flow of information and verbal exchange that demonstrated an easy command of technical vocabulary. It was no surprise to hear Philip, answering his questioners, speak about his ambition—to become an architect.

During this discussion, on my suggestion, the photographer, with perceptive observation, unobtrusively caught a moment when the individuality of each member of the group created a perfect composition.

It was many weeks later that the photograph reached me. Telephoning my thanks to the school, I learned that Philip had left. His "A" levels had not been of a sufficiently high grade for the school of architecture he wanted to enter. He had gone into a bank.

I asked if he could come out to see me as I wanted to have a tape-recording to go with the photograph. We recorded our discussion. This refocusing of attention on to his lost ambition had a decisive effect on him. "I realise," he said, "I'm in the wrong place; I'm going to leave the bank and go back to school to re-take my "A" levels and then I'll do the seven years' architecture course."

"And when you have done that, Philip, what would you hope to do?"

". . . I'd like to build a cathedral," he said, looking into the distance.

As teachers and examiners we, too, should be "building a cathedral". We should not regard "oracy" as a fragment in the curriculum but rather as a means whereby we can help to build, and assess, the *whole man*.

Personal Acknowledgements

In FIFTEEN years of this type of examining, I have had innumerable discussions with disciples and doubters, perfectionists and pragmatists, enthusiasts and enemies, to all of whom I should like to express my thanks.

I am especially grateful to Elizabeth Henry who convinced me that it was important that the book should be written and who at every stage in the development of English Speaking Board work has considered each detail in the light of sound educational philosophy. To Jocelyn Bell I tender my most sincere thanks for her patient listening, help in proofing and for her steadfast devotion to so many different projects which are the background experience contributing to this book.

All of us concerned with this work owe a debt of gratitude to Dr. Percy Hitchman for his arduous research into the techniques, methods and problems of oral examining and assessing. His book, *Examining Oral English in Schools*, published by Methuen, is a penetrating survey which gives every possible permutation of syllabus arrangement and methods of assessing, especially in the interviewer/interviewee situation. He has, over the years, shown interest in and given encouragement to the work of the English Speaking Board and we have had a constant interchange of ideas and experiences.

I also greatly appreciate the interest shown and encouragement given by Dr. W. A. Gatherer, H.M.I., who, while carrying out one of the largest single education authority tests for the city of Glasgow, found time to see and hear the different methods of E.S.B. and paid generous tributes to our work.

To the numerous H.M.I.s, heads of schools, principals of colleges, heads of departments fostering this work, the National Association for the Teaching of English—in particular Esmor Jones and Professor

G. C. Allen; the Regional Committees for the C.S.E.—and in particular F. Sparrow who played a leading role in the Southern Region tests carried out for the Schools Council and Dr. Andrew Wilkinson who considered all the elements of this work and presented a survey under the useful portmanteau word "oracy"—to all these I am indebted for their various reports, answers to questions, pamphlets, syllabuses and much written and oral exchange.

Outstanding in the field of those who have conducted major pioneering experiments and established examinations are Barbara Claypole who initiated the G.C.E. examinations in spoken English for the Joint Matriculation Board and the spoken English test of the Durham Board, and Arthur Wise who was primarily concerned with the establishment of the tests conducted by the University of Oxford and the University of Cambridge, being moderator for both. He was also Chief Examiner for the Durham test for eight years. Together he and Barbara Claypole initiated the London University "O" level G.C.E. test and became its first Chief Examiners. Their reports and writings have been eminently useful, based as they are on immense practical experience.

In conclusion I should like to commend and acknowledge the team of authors working on the SCOPE (Spoken Communication: an Open-plan Project in Education) series of books now in preparation for Pergamon Press. Through their zeal the many teaching methods obliquely suggested in this book are being presented in practical detail for each step of the Primary and Secondary school. At each stage of compilation we have exchanged manuscripts and shared thoughts.

All the people mentioned above, and many more, are injecting the teaching of English with life-blood. After all, what matters most is not the test itself but the teaching which precedes it. An imaginative and searching oral test could create and evaluate qualities which have too long been disregarded.

Acknowledgements and thanks are due to:

Lewis A. Partington for permission to reproduce photograph.
Philip Hamer and his friends who are the subjects in the photograph.
Laraine Gibbons, for her letter on The New Mersey Tunnel.

J. Lavery, her tutor, who guided her research.

Eunice Woodfield, for her contribution on the Sedgley Park College of Education.

Sister Thérèse Boddington, for her article on Notre Dame College of Education, Liverpool.

E. J. Burton, Head of the Drama Department, Trent Park College of Education, for his survey of B.Ed. speech and drama.

Basil Harvey, for his chapter on the examining of foreign students.

Her Majesty's Stationery Office.

The Times Educational Supplement (Astryx).

The Sunday Times (Maurice Wiggin).

The Guardian (John Grigg).

Messrs. Valentine & Sons, Ltd.

Messrs. Longmans, Green & Co., Ltd., Messrs. Barnes & Noble and F. D. Flower.

Messrs. Basil Blackwell Ltd. and Edna Mellor.

Joyce Finley for secretarial help and typing of the manuscript.

Norman Butterworth, Headmaster of Robert Bloomfield School, for help with proofs.

Ula Rigg and Audrey Price for permission to quote records of their students.

For Whom the Book Is Intended

THOUSANDS of teachers who have never had any training in the subject now find themselves involved in the teaching and examining of spoken English. In addition more and more teachers, as this work develops, will be expected to assess course work on an oral basis. Immense possibilities lie ahead so long as the preparation and the examination itself are both liberal and enriching.

Those who react against oral examinations will still find much in the book that will support and help them in their day to day teaching, for I have tried to look beyond examining to the educational philosophy underlying the methods.

The book also sets out to help specifically the large number of teachers of English who now find they are called on to act as internal or external examiners for the spoken English tests of the Certificate of Secondary Education. The advice should prove to be useful, too, to the many examiners engaged by the London Board for the G.C.E. "O" level tests in spoken English, especially the chapters on reading aloud and questions and conversation.

Next it is intended for those holding special English and Speech and Drama qualifications who wish to equip themselves as examiners for the English Speaking Board or other examining bodies specialising in the language arts.

Examiners already engaged in this field will find stimulus here to help them to refresh and reassess their examining technique and assessing ability. They will find that judgements have been defined and evaluated through the composite experience of other specialists and basic educational ideals have been empirically confirmed.

Teachers in training, whatever their specialisation, will discover the breadth of "oracy" for spoken English is treated as the common denominator of all subjects, the means whereby the questing mind shares discoveries and through this oral sharing is stimulated and challenged to further endeavour.

It is my belief that with progressive open-plan inter-disciplinary enquiry and team-teaching methods based on individual work-sheets and group projects, a written examination paper will not be enough for a true evaluation of a pupil's growth. The more natural culmination of this kind of learning should be oral reporting to the group, who, with the teacher as guide, will participate in and profit from searching dialogue.

There should also be important days in the school year when each member of the group presents to his colleagues some aspect of a subject which he has personally investigated and studied in depth. For as Madame Montessori said, long ago, of the child who has found the joy of complete absorption in his activity: "He detaches himself from the world in order to attain the power to unite himself with it."

CHRISTABEL BURNISTON

CHAPTER 1

The Scope and Stimulus of Oral Assessing

Why We Should Have Oral Exams in English

WE LIVE in an era of immense change in education where the very structure and content of the curriculum are being critically questioned and where "open-plan" team-teaching methods are giving a new impetus to learning. Therefore we must also consider new methods of *examining*.

It is also an age when teaching machines, films, audio-visual aids and computers can make a skilful job of imparting factual information. This gives the teacher a new role; on the one hand he must know the scope and the limitations of the apparatus available to him, on the other hand—and this applies to the English teacher more than any other—he must be actively concerned with the personal development, personal concord and personal relationships of all those in his care. All this comes back to the question of our speech, for it is on speech that our personal relationships depend. I make no apology for re-quoting the often-quoted dictum from the Newsom Report.

> There is no gift like the gift of speech and the level at which people have learned to use it determines the level of their companionship, the level at which their life is lived. *Half our Future* (Newsom Report).

> If this kind of examination (spoken English) led to schools paying more attention to oral work this would be one case where examinations were educationally beneficial. *Half our Future* (Newsom Report).

The only thing one would question in these admirable Newsom comments would be the word "gift". No one is born speaking. We absorb, listen, watch, imitate and experiment, using whoever happen to be around as our models for speech patterns. It is bad luck on a child if those models are inarticulate or aggressive, blurred or brash, stilted or strident, for he will imitate them with untiring repetition. And most of this untiring repetition will have happened before he comes to school. Every child, for good or ill, has had a pre-school course in speaking. This does not simplify the work of the teacher. It may complicate it. There are some primary schools where the French sounds the children hear and are making have more muscular energy, better tone and more precision than their English sounds. At this early stage, however, the muscles are beautifully flexible and there is a good chance of well-toned vital English speech developing if the teachers themselves have these qualities and can give an imaginative impulse for vital language response.

Thus, in the very early stages, care, guidance and practice must be given and sustained throughout school life. If spoken language is important enough to teach, it is important enough to *assess*; and the assessment itself can be both a target and a triggering-off for the next stage of enjoyable effort.

Although there have been examinations in speech and drama for the few, it is only since the Beloe Report and the subsequent introduction of the Certificate of Secondary Education that the matter has been given serious consideration for the main stream of education. All over the country syllabuses have been framed, tests have been tried out, regional committees have argued, English panels have thought and rethought, and unsure boys and girls have been "guinea-pigs" for unsure moderators and examiners. And from the prepared talks, impromptu talks, prepared readings, sight readings, conversations, discussions, aural comprehension tests, visual comprehension tests—either untaped or taped—has sprung an earnest complexity of post-mortems and reports.

So there is no lack of zealous intention, goodwill and effort. On the other hand, there is a restriction in the scope of the tests with the necessary watch on validity, objectivity and reliability, and consternation that 10 or 12 minutes of devoted personal attention must be given to each candidate.

But if we are to assess the full range of language, and not just the written word, what better way could there be of using our time? For we must show in a practical way that the *spoken* word is the medium by which we communicate. In the world outside school and college the written word takes a secondary place. If this is true of the utility jobs we have to do, it is still more true that personal relationships and our attitude and adjustment to our environment depend on the quality, subtlety and range of our spoken language.

It might be argued, why have an *examination*? Surely we can take it for granted that our children can talk? And if they are not articulate will not an examination simply expose their weaknesses and make them even more awkward and inhibited? These questions must not be dismissed lightly. After many years of examining spoken English, my fellow examiners of the English Speaking Board would agree with me that quite the worst time to *introduce* a spoken English test is in the final years of secondary school life when, unless there has been constant and encouraging education in movement and speech, the adolescent is likely to be excessively self-conscious. What, indeed, can boys and girls of 15 or 16 do about it, if they are so linguistically limited that they are marked Grade D or E or worse still "ungraded" in the C.S.E. examination in their final year of school? Who will be there, as they turn their backs on the school walls, to help them?

So we must begin at the beginning. This is difficult indeed when the peak time for the reception of language is before school life starts. But let us begin where we can, with the reception class in the infants' school, with the first "Good-morning!", through all their activity and play, meals and milk and so on through every subsequent year of infant, junior and secondary school life. Nothing less will do. Only if we have done this have we earned the right to examine our children in spoken English. We must give them guidance and practice at every stage, and in every lesson. This can only be achieved by much more comprehensive training in oral methods in the colleges of education, whatever the subject discipline the teacher is pursuing.

What Are We Examining?

Having accepted the introduction of spoken English examinations and having put them in motion, we must still ask ourselves: WHAT is being examined?

This throws us back to an analysis of what is contained in oral teaching in general, and oral English in particular, for spoken English belongs to all subjects and therefore its frontiers almost defy definition. It is a highly subjective affair and cannot be divorced from the total personality. Further, unlike the other subjects in the curriculum the child's parents and his kinship group will have contributed more to the sum total of the child's linguistic ability than all the teachers in his school.

No person can communicate in isolation: any success in the use of language is dependent on the quality of the *listener* and his response. We cannot, therefore, examine "a candidate" as a separate entity; we can only examine his reaction with others as a listener and a speaker. Communication changes in quality and kind for every different speech situation and therefore we should provide in each examination certain situations which do not depend on the initiative of the interviewer. If, for example, the oral examination is solely a verbal exchange between examiner and candidate with the examiner initiating the talk, it might well be that the candidate's failure reflects the *examiner's* failure to create the right stimulus or follow a clue which would lead to a genuine response and spontaneous language flow.

Those are just a few of the psychological problems we must face in planning our examinations.

What Are We Examining Technically?

Primarily we are concerned with communication and not with derivative or imitative public speaking or recitation.

We are not setting narrow judgements on "standard English" or "received pronunciation". (The English Speaking Board has recordings of young people living in different parts of the United Kingdom and from a wide social range; each speaker is recognisable as representative of his region but it would be generally conceded that each speaker has good spoken English.)

However, we must resist the present tendency to condone mumbled, hesitant, ill-formed speech as being "sincere and natural". It is part of the British temperament to regard attention to speech as an affectation; consequently some arid and formless talk is accepted as being relaxed or spontaneous.

It is important, therefore, to set out the total responsibility of the teacher of spoken English and the consequent involvement of the examiner.

1. Through a wide range of activity and oral expression extending very often beyond the school walls, we must help our children:

(a) to adjust themselves to their environment (meeting people, shopping, travelling, etc.);

(b) to receive and impart information on their basic skills (school subjects, hobbies, tasks at home, in clubs, etc.);

(c) to encourage courteous and happy relationships with members of the family, school and extended kinship groups;

(d) to make their own discoveries and enquiries and report them with oral confidence (environmental studies, visits to public libraries, museums, factories, etc.);

(e) to interpret and communicate the printed word so that literature is not only enjoyed intellectually but actively (poetry, prose, scripted drama, the novel and short story);

(f) to free the body and heighten the imagination so that there is a spontaneous creative oral response (e.g. creative drama, original writing, verbal dynamics, etc.);

(g) to become responsive *listeners* who react with sensibility to those they meet in the situations arising in (a) to (f) and are intelligent critics of radio, television, film and theatre.

2. To do this adequately the young must be given stimulus and guidance in:

(a) making their own discoveries;

(b) thinking clearly about their discoveries;

(c) putting their thoughts into spoken words;

(d) arranging words in an orderly and acceptable form;

(e) giving this form meaningful rhythm (pace, pressure and pause);

(f) giving these thoughts meaningful cadence with a free and flexible voice (physical vocal security, well-toned and imaginatively ranged);

(g) giving these thoughts clarity with toned-up muscles of the speech instrument (neat articulation, enunciation and forward projection);

(h) communicating thoughts through the non-verbal elements of speech (significant and sincere facial expression and meaningful movement).

What Form Should the Examination Take?

Obviously the oral test which has the most far-reaching influence is the one that includes speech situations which touch, in some way, the different planes of interaction as set out in 2(a)–(h). The examination, while keeping close to the child's experience and immediate concerns, must also stimulate verbal response at a higher level of experience and should, therefore, include some literature, preferably of the child's own choice, which is evocative, stimulating and memorable (see Chapter 5).

The test should be designed in such a way that the speaker is in *authority*. This means that he should be allowed to talk on some subject he has lived with for several weeks or even months making discoveries from his own investigations. If each child in the group has been actively occupied on his independent quests the day of assessment can be one of genuine reporting and sharing and not a tedious repetition of an already delivered "lecturette" (see Chapter 3).

It is implicit, therefore, in such an examination that there is a listening, participating group. This, as will be shown later in the book, is not a group of candidates "waiting to be heard", but individuals, who may at any moment be questioners, people receiving instructions, resistant customers, critical viewers, contributors to some communal plan, opposers or proposers in some discussion, agitators for some local improvement or simply listeners of sensibility sharing some aesthetic experience. The main point is that none of the situations will be contrived; they will arise from the immediate issues and come from genuine enquiry (see Chapter 6).

We also believe in the great value of reading aloud, not as a sight reading, which may be on a subject that is of no interest to the reader, but rather a passage chosen from a book which has been *enjoyed* and which should hold the attention of the listening group (see Chapter 4).

CHAPTER 2

The Framework of the English Speaking Board Tests

General Form of the Syllabus

1. *Personal project.* This should be a spontaneously delivered section of a carefully prepared and extended study. Visual aids and relevant gear of any kind may accompany the exposition (3 minutes). (See Chapter 3.)
2. *Reading aloud.* The candidate brings a book he has *enjoyed* and must be prepared to communicate that enjoyment to the listening group. The examiner will select a passage and probably ask for some elucidation of a certain idea or character (not more than 2 minutes). (See Chapter 4.)
3. *Own choice.* In the E.S.B. syllabus are several suggestions (related to the candidate's mental development) from which he may make a choice of poetry, prose or drama. In the "entry" grade (which any new candidate of any age may take) the "own choice" is entirely the candidate's. In this section we encourage original writing, group acting, etc. Where a group present drama, they can use the collected time of the relevant number of candidates (2 minutes each). (See Chapter 5.)
4. Questions, discussion or impromptu extensions arising at any time from 1, 2 and 3. In this section a part or whole of the listening group will be particularly involved. (See Chapter 6.)

If an examination is to be constructive it should give the maximum scope for the candidate's personal experience and potentiality. It is implicit in such a premise that a good examination improves the quality and kind of teaching.

It is true to say that where E.S.B. examinations have been prepared by teachers working on the fringe of the school activity (private lessons by visiting teachers, where the subject is treated as a "frill", or if the teacher is in the main stream of education but is working without the support of others on the staff) these criteria are rarely met. On the other hand, it has been interesting to see that many examinations which began in this way have gradually drawn in other members of staff and affected every school activity.

Where E.S.B. philosophy has been integrated into school life the effect of the examinations is most marked. We now know children who took a Junior Introductory Certificate at the age of 7 or 8 and have taken a further grade each year of their school life. We have witnessed a marked growth in confidence, extension of vocabulary and structure of English; imaginative response to literature; linking of English with every other subject in the school and beyond it, and increased sense of social responsibility.

How Are We Examining?

Physical Arrangements

The arrangement of the room for E.S.B. examinations is sometimes outside our control, but in our instructions to organisers of examinations we do ask for a room without desks. The chairs should be arranged in such a way that no listener is very far away from the speaker and the speaker should be in the position of authority—not the examiner. It is helpful to place the examiner slightly to one side of the speaker and as part of the audience. In this way he does not dominate the situation but is in a strategic position to link the candidate and his listeners, for he can address both. A horse-shoe arrangement of chairs is more friendly than straight rows and adds to the intimacy of the occasion, giving the speaker importance without projecting him into an area of isolation.

Props, Visual Aids, etc.

We encourage the candidates to help one another both before and during the examination in courteous "stage-managing". Candidates who are practised in E.S.B. procedure or in reporting orally in their own courses ensure that posters, maps, graphs or pictures are already on boards for quick display. The more unwieldy gear is speedily set out with the help of one or two colleagues. However, there is no reason why examiners should not co-operate with the schools or technical colleges by moving in to the appropriate workshop, chemistry laboratory or domestic science room if the candidates are explaining some kind of technical process.

When Should the Examination Take Place?

A head of a school or head of an English department is naturally concerned about the amount of time such an examination will take. We recommend that the traditional peak examination periods should be avoided. There is no need for a speech assessment to be in the last term of the school year. It could be taken at any time. Some schools have adopted the E.S.B. type of test but have it internally marked, and spread the items of the syllabus into different terms. This simplifies the teaching programme and the days when projects are heard can be "open-days" where there is interchange of staff and classes so that the speakers have a change of audience. This keeps the subjects and the occasion fresh and introduces different sections of the school to one another in lively activity. This is not waste of time; it is a most fruitful way of using it. Even if the examination is taken as a whole we should not begrudge the speaker 12 minutes intensive hearing, for simultaneously a whole group of listeners profit from his experience and the exchange of ideas.

Who Is to Examine?

Our experience so far would suggest that the best examiners usually possess both English and speech qualifications. Some of our examiners however, are qualified on one side only but through the years have acquired special knowledge and have had wide experience in the various aspects of English teaching. We select our examiners not only for their qualifications but for their temperaments and personalities, for the job is very exacting. In addition, we in the E.S.B. choose examiners from our panel who are most suited for the particular age-group and the particular social background. A good examiner in an industrial technical college would not necessarily be successful with young children in a country school. Obviously there are not enough people of this kind to cope with the huge number of candidates taking the C.S.E. examinations.

London University G.C.E. Examining Board threw the net wide and certainly managed to find qualified and experienced people for their marathon G.C.E. "O" level test. Though they differed considerably in the type of training and their respective qualifications, they all had specialist teaching of one kind or another. However, with skilful co-ordinating meetings and clear instructions from the chief examiners, this interviewer/interviewee type of test (sight-reading and conversation) has been successfully launched and neatly administered. It is an examination which it is tempting to emulate since it can be organised a good deal more tidily than other spoken English tests and is certainly more manageable in terms of examiner training.

Ideally one ought to be able to assume that all teachers of English should be good teachers of *spoken* English and potentially good examiners. Of course there are many such English teachers . . . there are also four-leaved clovers!

If standards are to be raised we must start at many points. One of the immediate needs is to have in-service training courses for teachers and potential examiners. There is hope for the more distant future. A few colleges of education are now having specialist courses in speech and drama, and the candidates taking a four-year course for the B.Ed. degree with English and Spoken English and Drama as main subjects should have a relevant basic training. However, they would also need to have many years' teaching and some specialised training as examiners before they would have the necessary authority.

Qualities and Techniques of Examiners

Given this special training and experience, what qualities and techniques should one expect of an examiner of oral subjects in the group situation?

1. He must genuinely like people.
2. He must show it.
3. His voice and speech should have clarity and vitality.
4. He must have wide interests himself, and be receptive to the interests and enthusiasms of others.
5. He must treat each individual individually and—this is most important—as a *social asset*.

6. He should tune in to the candidate, gently building up the nervous and diffident and perhaps deflecting attention from the glib or the aggressive.

7. He must not come with preconceived ideas of "steering" but should be ready to follow a track to a point where the candidate can expand his ideas.

8. He must listen because he is sincerely interested and not just because he is an examiner.

9. He must ask questions from genuine enquiry and not with the intention of exposing gaps in knowledge.

10. Yet he must question searchingly so that the candidate goes deeper into the thinking process.

11. He must frame his questions in such a way that the candidate has to take over and develop the point.

12. He must, unless he suspects lack of effort, respect the candidate's choice of material even though he may think it is immature or second rate. He can make suggestions for the next stage and thus give oblique criticism which encourages the speaker to raise his standards.

13. He must be quick to sense the kind of speech situation which could arise from the material presented to him. This may be designed to help the candidate to overcome some weakness or to meet a different challenge.

14. He must notice if the candidate has any undue muscular tension, and give opportunity for release. This is best done by giving the muscles a purposeful job, e.g. active demonstration, pointing out details in the visual aids, etc.

15. He must, throughout the examination, by the way he introduces the items and draws interest and questions from the *audience*, completely involve them as responsive listeners interacting with the speakers.

16. He must create a bouyant atmosphere of enjoyable "sharing" and sustain it so that the last candidate is given the same welcome and pleasant oral exchange as the first.

17. He must (for E.S.B. exams) write brief comments of *constructive* criticism which will be understood by the candidate and the teacher.

CHAPTER 3

Personal Projects for the Spoken English Test

There are, in any case, some objectives which can and ought deliberately to be pursued through every part of the curriculum. Very high in this list we should place improvement in powers of speech; not simply improvement in the quality and clearness of enunciation, although that is needed, but a general extension of vocabulary, and, with it, a surer command over the structures of spoken English and the expression of ideas. That means seizing the opportunity of every lesson, in engineering or housecraft or science as well as in English, to provide material for discussion—genuine discussion; not mere testing by teacher's question and pupil's answer. (Newsom Report).

Even as a child, every human being should be treated as a necessary essential of humanity. (Froebel.)

What Is a Personal Project?

First of all, perhaps, it is important to define what we mean by "personal project" and perhaps the simplest way is to say what it is not.

It is not a lecturette mugged-up from a nearby textbook; it is not a superficial talk where a speaker tells all he knows; it is not a spoken essay where he translates a written composition into vocal terms. It is not a test in imitative public speaking where a too-large subject is reduced to note-headings and a stilted form of language. It is none of these. We can find our clues to what it is in the quotations which initiate this chapter.

First it must be concerned with the person's own skills, discoveries, enquiries and interests. It may be essentially practical and involve the co-ordination of hand and brain as well as an oral exposition; it may be the explanation of some scientific process which the speaker demonstrates, or it may be a focusing on to some small area of a field study investigated in detail. Whatever the project, the maps, models and relevant gear should be boldly shown and treated as an integral part of the talk. With this approach, spoken English becomes the meeting ground for all the various disciplines and delights—a reporters' symposium. Each member of the group is treated as an equally valuable member of society, the boy who has learnt to use the potter's wheel is not considered inferior to the boy who writes Latin verse. As Froebel says, each one is "an essential member of humanity".

The Candidate in Authority

If this is true, then the teacher or examiner must put the pupil in a position of authority. The teacher does this in the first place by setting high standards himself in his own researches and in directing the pupils to make their own discoveries. He constantly shows the pupil how to track things down and how to consult authoritative sources. When the pupil has made his *own* notes, written his *own* letters, telephoned his *own* enquiries, made his *own* diagrams, he has built understanding into himself and he can speak with authority. The examiner's business is to treat him as "the one who knows", not as a candidate to be tripped up. In such circumstances there is a genuine desire to communicate, indeed an urgency. In preparing such a project, and from it extracting material for a 3-minute talk, the speaker meets many challenges: he must marshal his material and select logically and scientifically; he must arrange the material in the sequence which will clarify the subject for his listeners; he must deal with technical terms and elucidate them; he must adapt his timing and delivery for his particular audience. Subsequently, when the 3-minute talk is complete, he must answer questions in informal conversational exchange with his colleagues and the examiner. It is *his* arena and he can use it just as he pleases to put his subject across. He will be left in no doubt at all as to whether he has held the attention of his listeners. The young will not make the histrionic effort to disguise boredom even though the examiner may! Here is the supreme opportunity for the candidate (or in class the pupil/reporter) to be able to communicate private and specialist enthusiasms to an assorted selection of listeners. Through their questions he will have to clarify and amplify any points in the talk and possibly give a physical demonstration of or instruction on some particular process.

"Topic", "Project" or "Interdisciplinary Enquiry"?

In the Southern Region report on C.S.E. testing-method II: the prepared talk, the distinction between a true personal project and an arbitrarily contrived "topic" can be deduced.

> A considerable number spoke on topics they knew little or nothing about. The impression given in these cases was that the subjects had been "mugged-up" for the occasion. It is the teacher's responsibility to guide children to speak on topics in which they are really interested. Two examples of this were a talk on Bream fishing by a candidate of average intelligence and one on a visit to the Abstract Art Exhibition at the Tate Gallery by a very intelligent girl.

The point to be made here is, one would think, that the boy had actually handled a rod and had *contended* with the bream. He did not give a theoretical talk on "Fishing". The girl, too, had been to the Tate Gallery—seen for herself and drawn her own conclusions on Abstract Art.

Experience and Language

In each case it is the experience itself which produces the relevant colourful and precise vocabulary.

Again in the Southern Region report the examiner comments on the general inability to communicate and the "lack of vocabulary experience". Here the operative word is "experience". We must experience language. Let me put it this way:

Words do not carry meanings like the ceramic-chain labels on decanters, for they can only have a precise meaning in their own context. Therefore we should never teach vocabulary in a vacuum; rather we should extend the experience, the enquiry or the activity so that words have a living relevance. For example, what very different images are conjured up by the word GROUP in the minds of: an educationist; a psychologist; an evangelist; an adolescent; a guitar player; a statistician; an income-tax collector or now a reader of paper backs? Similarly the word FIGURE has a different technical connotation for the tailor; the mathematician; the printer; the musician; the dancer; the skater and the sculptor. What does the word RANK suggest to a soldier; a film agent; an examiner; a gardener; a perfumier; a baker; an aristocrat? In each case the meaning is entirely different depending on the different register in which it is used.

Finding the Experience

In a secondary school where I was examining, a 15-year-old boy gave a splendid talk on the solar system with clear, bold diagrams and spontaneous blackboard drawings. When he had finished his talk, the questions came freely and probingly from the audience who were keen to know more. Where there were alternative opinions he was able to refer his questioner to a well-selected bibliography and quoted, too, from his own telescopic observations. I made the comment that he must have been preparing his talk for a long time because the subject had obviously been studied in depth. "Yes," he answered reflectively, "I've really been preparing it for seven years". In such a case there was no poverty of vocabulary. His desire to communicate, which had not been stifled in class, caused his explanatory English to keep pace with his remarkable technical expertise.

The value of this wide and thorough choice of subject is most marked in the scope it gives the non-academic boy and girl. Here is a chance for someone who has enthusiastically and faithfully followed some pursuit to "share" it with his fellows. As Carlyle said, "It is certain my conviction gains infinitely the moment another soul will believe in it". There is much more stimulus in talking about one's own enthusiasms than in writing it all down. Let me give an example of a situation where writing would certainly not be the appropriate medium. In a secondary school in Scotland, a fifth-year girl presented for her personal project the theme: "My evolution as a pianist." For the talk she sat at the grand piano and began "When I was five . . ." As she grew in age, in her 3-minute talk, so she developed in technique and complexity of vocabulary, illustrating her words with a few selected bars of music to demonstrate the various stages. She finished with an extract from a piano concerto. Here was a girl who had been by-passed when selections were made for grammar school entry, whose talents and industry went far beyond the school walls.

In a school in the south a group of fifth-form boys talked on their particular instruments in the school orchestra; after the individual projects they joined together in a short ensemble playing.

Where the examiner feels that the visual aid is doing most of the communicating for the candidate, it is quite easy to interrupt for a more detailed elucidation of a particular point. But we do find that through the handling of gear and demonstrating, the candidate is physically released and involved; the eye focus is freer and more significant because the candidate looks at his listeners and his props in genuine explanation.

How to Avoid the "Spoken Essay"

This really goes back to the type of teaching. If the pupil is really investigating and the enquiry approach to learning is habitual, the pupil will rarely be rehearsing a talk in class but will be reporting progress. He will also be making various written accounts, reports, minutes and letters which go far beyond his final oral précis. If the teacher is being consulted by thirty other pupils he will be too busy guiding and answering questions to hear talks being "recited". In any case the day of presentation and assessment should be a rewarding experience for all those concerned if every project in its final phase is new to the listeners. If it is not, then it is up to the examiner to divert the speaker from the notes or memorised phrases. It is interesting to hear how the speaker's voice becomes warmer and better ranged in the true "finding" of thought when he abandons his stilted essay.

The choice of subject often in itself determines the style and quality of the talk and the degree of spontaneity. We always recommend that the candidate narrows the area of a subject down so that he can study it in depth and show his personal research and experiences. One of the C.S.E. panels asks that a talk should be prepared which is in no way autobiographical. We feel that such a direction is a major error for it may lead to the speaker giving second-hand textbook knowledge. Other panels suggest subjects for impromptu talks and give broad titles which may lead the speaker into a woolly tangle of vague generalisations or a hollow formal structure.

Looking down one list of "topics" presented by C.S.E. candidates one finds: Education; Advertising; The Commonwealth; Canada, U.S.A.; France; Africa; Music. Surely no one, let alone a boy or girl of 15, should *presume* to talk on such topics in three minutes.

A true personal project may be connected with one of the above subjects but the talk will be on a particularised aspect chosen and investigated by the pupil himself. For example:

Not "Education" but "Why I believe in co-education";

Not "Advertising" but "Resisting the Television commercials";

Not "The Commonwealth" but "Searching for semi-precious stones with my father in Tanganyika";

Not "Canada" but "My uncle's work in lumbering";

Not "U.S.A." but "President Kennedy: the champion of the youth of the world";

Not "France" but "Working in the Burgundy vineyards";

Not "Africa" but "Manners and customs in Kenya";

Not "Music" but "Playing in the National Youth Orchestra".

I hope I am not seeming to suggest that the talker should always have visual aids. Some of the most moving and compelling subjects have been exclusively personal experiences which involved the speaker emotionally or were concerned with family relationships. On one occasion a girl gave a perceptive account of her family life with a mentally deficient brother. It was hard to believe that the wise comments were coming from a secondary modern schoolgirl of only 15, for she showed how every member of her family was enriched by this particular relationship. Step by step she analysed the boy's development and pointed out how each member of the family contributed to it. As an observer at this examination reported: "In the space of a few minutes a whole new outlook on life was revealed for everyone in the room. In a rare moment of communication one sensed that for every child and adult present life would never be quite the same again."

Another girl gave a detailed account of her mother's work as a foster parent: "When Daphne came my mother had to burn all her clothes. . . ." In brief verbal cameos she brought each foster child to life and in every case, however difficult, her mother's loving enthu-

siasm for each one of them shone through. We heard how the large
family of parents, children and foster children every year mended
and made toys for Christmas for those who would not have them;
details were given of each child's allotted task.

Another 17-year-old girl in a secondary school told of how she and
her friends started a holiday play centre for young school children
whose mothers were working. Every detail of costing—menus,
apparatus, division of the day—had been carefully worked out. The
children were in no sense merely "being minded", but were actively
engaged in creative play: painting, modelling, building, etc. This
was not a flash-in-the-pan effort but had already been sustained
over three holiday periods. Their chief worry was their waiting list.
Such accounts are mental jolts for everyone in the audience. At
these times we find we are examining ourselves.

Open-plan Projects

Here are a few examples taken from scores of other projects presented in the E.S.B. exams which took the candidates far beyond the
school walls and made them have to deal with many situations in
oral exchange.

(a) *How coal gas is made.* The boy concerned worked at the gas-
works in the holidays. In the pursuit of his project he asked for and
was granted interviews with the production manager, foremen,
technicians and labourers and trade union officials. He made
enquiries about the latest modifications in machinery and wrote for
information to works outside his own town. He made large precise
diagrams showing the function of the machinery and demonstrated
this during his talk. From these experiences alone he had learnt a
great deal about how to "tune in" to various types of people, to
draw out information from them and to collate it in a logical order. It
is impossible to convey the vitality and breadth of this particular talk.

(b) *The picture post-card industry.* This seemed at first sight to be
rather an elementary choice of subject for a girl at "O" level. In fact
it had opened out a new world for her. From being an inhibited shy
girl she developed a great deal of confidence and poise in the pursuit
of this single project. The initial breakthrough was a series of letters
to the manager of the Valentine Company in Dundee who gave her

most valuable information on the history of the picture post-cards and sent her samples of their many designs. She became so interested, and grew so much in confidence, that she saved up her own money and arranged to travel from Aberdeen to Dundee and spend a day in the works. This involved her in interviews and interrogation of production managers, designers, artists, printers and the keeper of the archives. She then collated it and condensed it into a 3-minute report. After her 3-minute talk to a group of her contemporaries, she could have answered questions for an hour. This was probably the first time in her life that she had become, and been treated as, an "authority".

(c) *The School founder, Lady Olivia Sparrow.* In the pursuit of this project the girl wrote numerous letters of enquiry and made personal and telephone calls to the local art galleries, museums and descendants of the Sparrow family. She proudly displayed on the day of her examination a neat stack of letters which had resulted from her enquiries. When letters are to be posted and answers received there is an incentive to try for perfection in composition, spelling and calligraphy. Through this one project the girl had grown in social relationships, poise, courtesy, written and spoken English and historical knowledge.

With such diverse material where every subject in the school curriculum is involved and where the child with an absorbing hobby may have an advantage, how are we to assess? Where does the magnetic needle come to rest when, for example, it is drawn to the credit side on the content of the talk and to the debit side on a poor delivery and lack of audience contact? If we can remember that primarily and finally the assessment is on *communication*, then we can justify a decision which may put a girl who has given a clear, attractive verbal commentary and demonstration of a fairly simple topic such as "Flower arrangement", in the B category, and another who has given a dull but well-informed dissertation on "Reproduction in the Pandorina colony", in the C category. The quality of the listening may suggest the answer. We can ask: "What will the listeners *remember*?"

Perhaps if we take a selection at random from a score of reports on examinations from the personal project section of the C.S.E. pilot tests by E.S.B., it may help to show the various factors which the

3

examiner is considering. In each of the following cases the candidate would, in an E.S.B. examination, be given a more helpful written report.

The following summing up was for the school's record and the interest of the moderators:

Choice of Personal Projects

The personal projects ranged through the functional, artistic, sporting, social—all aspects of life were touched. The first boy spoke on the school "Wall newspaper" of which he was editor, and although obviously he had the authority to speak on the subject, since he was personally involved in it, he had memorised an essay word for word. The examiner led through questions and those of the listening group to a more full and true communication. The speakers on "The motor bicycle" and "Impressionist painters" both weakened in communication because they had only a superficial knowledge of their subjects. The glib speaker was even less effective than the floundering one. Sometimes an unusual subject, e.g. "Antique guns and shooting", was entertaining, had an interesting "visual aid", but was disorganised in thinking. However, more demands were made on his vocabulary and flow of thought than, for example, the speaker who showed (without any actual manipulation) her "Plastic modelling kit", a childish hobby for a fifth-year girl. "Puppetry" and "Heraldry" were skilfully communicated by both speakers, with impeccable visual aids, the second especially showed that when a subject has been truly pursued, there is a resultant enrichment of personal vocabulary. A talk on "Pop music" was a very much more mature assessment and comment than comparable talks in other schools on this subject, but the girl who talked on "My musical education" was a splendid example of how practical grappling with an art and the necessary muscular discipline can enrich the whole personality and personal vocabulary. Another aspect of "sound" was dealt with in a talk somewhat drily called "The use of the tape-recorder". In struggling to find words to try to express his incredulity and delight at receiving such a present, he communicated perfectly. (Here was an example of where a formal "taping" of a talk would have missed the glowing facial expression and the searching pauses.) Other talks: "My holidays abroad", "Acting in a school play", "Are books a waste of time?", "Giving a successful party" all had grace and charm.

But the talks which really were communicated in the fullest sense of the word were "My ski-ing holiday" and "Hairdressing". In both these talks the girls assumed from the start that what they had to say was worth saying and that we were worth addressing. The former speaker gave practical graphic instruction in which her whole body was alive and expressive. This spontaneity of words sprang from the essential physical directness and freedom. Rhythm of speech was geared to give time for the audience to see, hear and receive. Language was dynamic because it was correlated to movement. The second girl was so obviously enthusiastic and professional in her attitude to her job that we could anticipate her future success with people and her high professional standards.

Very often candidates were steered away from stereotyped delivery in the informal part of the test; for example, the girl who gave the talk on "Giving a successful party" was asked to welcome three of her colleagues (who actually went outside the door), introduce them to one another and initiate the first conversation. This was carried out with social ease and clarity.

To sum up (and this is true of other schools and areas), the weaker candidates fell short in communicating because of:

(a) lack of information, therefore a lack of authority, e.g. "The motor cycle";

(b) lack of intellectual integrity, e.g. "The Impressionists";

(c) rigidity in delivery—the "spoken essay" technique, e.g. "The Wall newspaper";

(d) lack of projection or vocal vitality, e.g. "The history of Association Football".

Factors to be taken into account in the judging of the personal project are:

Quality of the content

Clarity of arrangement

Extent and richness of vocabulary

Method of presentation

Relevance of and reference to the visual aids

Audience contact and involvement

Personal enthusiasm

Spontaneity and sincerity

Timing for audience reception

Quality of voice and articulation

As in all other sections of the examination it is useful for the examiner to assume that the candidate is "average" until he proves otherwise. If one is working on a five-letter or number category A B C D E, then one can start with the magnetic needle, as it were, in the C category. Factors on the debit side will swing the needle to the right, but there may be compensating factors pulling over to the left. Although, as in all the other sections, the examiner is giving an "impression" mark, it is arrived at, in the case of an experienced examiner, from a number of particular points within the whole. E.S.B. examiners are advised not to be concerned with marking to the detriment of their listening. Genuine listening and a spontaneous impression mark are much more likely to give a reliable assessment than nervous fidgeting with letters and numbers prompted by an ear which is merely listening for faults, and an eye which is giving no help to the candidate.

In order to get the "feel" of assessment (but certainly not to suggest any slavish commitment to the separate comments in the diagram) a grouping of possible categories is set out below. Obviously there are many more points to consider than those suggested in the wedge-shape divisions. The ones chosen are simply there as a possible guide. The varying size of the respective grade divisions suggests the proportion of candidates, on a national basis, which would normally be allocated to that particular grade.

Suggested qualities which are being measured in the candidate's talk on a personal project

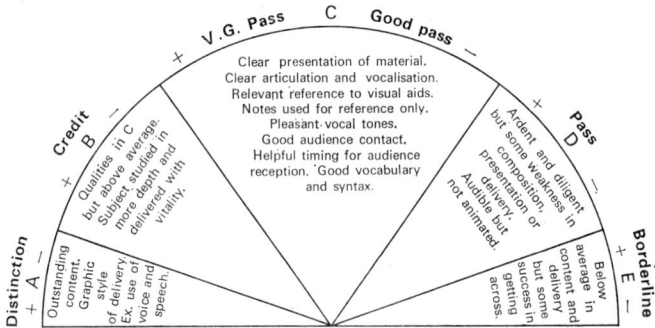

If the candidate is marked "Ungraded" or "Fail" he will have proved to be unsuccessful in formulating and communicating ideas.

Obviously varying degrees of success in any one component will determine the final grading; for example, a talk which might be rather loose in construction might succeed completely because of its spontaneity and vitality. A subject which was undemanding in research might have involved the candidate in practical manual work and be successfully communicated through verbal commentary combined with physical demonstration.

The examiner must not be influenced by any predetermined academic grouping. There are many kinds of intelligence; the most academically able may prove to be limited in oral communication and in making agreeable social contacts.

CHAPTER 4

Reading Aloud

Has the Subject any Value as an Oral Test?

There has been much discussion amongst people concerned with the formulation of spoken English tests about the advisability of using reading aloud as a basis for examination, or even for part of the test. Attitudes are diametrically opposed. For example, whereas the London University G.C.E. Board bases its whole spoken English test on the reading of a formerly unseen passage (presented by the examiner 10 minutes before the audition), the Southern Region, after its pilot C.S.E. tests, criticised reading aloud as a possible method of assessment because the results were so poor!

After pointing out, quite rightly, that "no decent reading can be performed unrehearsed" it suspects that a rehearsed reading could be imposed by the teacher. The Southern Region committee felt that a specialist oral examination in English literature had no place in a GENERAL examination of this kind. In the summing up of comments by the examiner and a colleague observer a sad conclusion is reached:

> We gained little from the reading aloud. It told us nothing new about the power of communication, and it offered little as a subject of discussion, for most of the examinees had small interest in the books they brought for reading, nor were they able to comment fruitfully upon them.

and later:

> Reading was very bad on the whole, and the question arose: "Was reading skill part of the examination and a factor to influence marking, or was the reading purely a means of establishing a talking point?"

One can imagine from those few words the frustration and tedium which the examiners endured, however well disguised, and the discomfiture of the candidates, apparently totally ignorant of what was expected of them. The examiners were unfortunately having to see and hear the result of ten years' neglect of literature which should be at the very heart of our living.

So we are driven to ask: Why had the candidates "small interest in the books they brought?" Why were they not able "to comment fruitfully upon them"? We cannot blame the children, since there are hundreds of children not necessarily specially gifted whose lives have been enriched because literature has come alive for them. Are we then to cut out reading aloud because it has not been taught? Should we not take these examiners' comments seriously and bring back into school life this skill, which Hilaire Belloc said was as good a test as any of the well-educated man?

The careful investigations carried out by the Southern Region and the Schools Council should make us examine the whole quality of teaching of English in general and the teaching of reading in particular, for if children are deprived, at any stage in their lives, of literature appropriate to their interest and ability and reading skill, will they not be stunted in linguistic, aesthetic, emotional and social growth?

Importance and Scope of Reading Aloud

We must therefore make reading important; it must be both wide and intense, serious and light-hearted, silent and spoken. The stimulus which is most likely to excite a child's own desire to read is hearing, from an early age, nursery rhymes, songs, stories, fables, myths, historical accounts, episodes in the Bible and poetry, spoken by adults with spacious imaginations and reading skill.

The teacher should set an example here. If stories, poems and plays to be read in class are prepared with the same care that an actor would give a script for a public reading, the young audience will subconsciously absorb the idea that the interpretation of an author's words is a trust which must not be broken. The teacher should so establish himself as the supreme story-teller that there is a ripple of delight through the class the moment he opens the book. We English Speaking Board assessors who have visited all types of schools in the United Kingdom can recall many schools where children have become different people because of the right kind of English teaching (not only English, of course). Five schools which come into my mind, in a quick selection from many more, could not be more different: one is a large public boarding school for girls in a cathedral city in the west; the second is a secondary modern school in a rural area in the east; the third is a church school in a condemned building in an industrial town in the north; the fourth is a primary school in residential suburbia in the midlands; the fifth is a massive comprehensive school in a Scottish city. The social backgrounds, regional pronunciation and working environment of all these schools are entirely different but in each case there is a teacher who has brought literature to life and language to the lips. The contribution that these teachers make to the personal development of the young people in their care cannot be measured.

In such schools, as in most others, the dreary business of reading-round-the-class has long since been abandoned. Here the children consider it a privilege, not a chore, to be one of the readers in the well-planned-ahead English lesson. A few days living with the selected passage, discovering the meaning of the words and the right pronunciation, a run through aloud in spare time, assure that "on the day" the listening group can go far beyond aural comprehension to a real absorption of the writer's thoughts and style. The poor reader can be given a shorter passage and longer time for preparing it and have prearranged listening help from a more able colleague. Once he has achieved success and been spared the misery of oral struggle in public he will have the necessary incentive to read on his own and, with plenty of time for preparation, read again later to his group.

In this kind of school where people care about people, one hears in assembly, speaking and reading of the Bible and secular literature arranged and presented by the pupils themselves which does, indeed, lift the heart. In one such school the older pupils work to a high standard of reading aloud for the privilege of visiting the lower classes to tell them stories. None of this just happens. In each school where there is this kind of generosity and rapport, a first-class English teacher is at the heart of things. On these occasions, sometimes simple, occasionally spectacular, there is a coming together, on all sides, of many kinds of faithfulness.

Raising the Standard of Reading

How are we then to raise the standard? First of all we must reinstate reading, and I mean reading *aloud*, as an important part of education. It has been neglected for too long. This is not to decrease the amount of silent reading; it will in fact increase it, since all reading will become more meaningful because aural perception is sharpened. If we are dealing with literature which is well written—and there should be no place in our schools for anything that is not—it will have a compulsive rhythm and dynamic dialogue which demands either an actual vocal interpretation or a silently imagined one. Without this flexibility of pace, pitch, tone and pause the printed word is as immobilised as an uninterpreted musical score.

One way of giving reading aloud the necessary status is to make it a part of the spoken English test.

In the English Speaking Board system we stipulate in section 3 of the four-part examination that the candidate should bring to the examination a book he has *enjoyed* and be prepared to communicate his enjoyment to the listening group. Usually while the examiner is selecting the short passage, he asks for some specific information to be given to put the audience in the picture. This is always a genuine linking of speaker and listener. Comments are exchanged which show a shared interest. If, however, the book is unfamiliar to the examiner, there is genuine enquiry. In this way both listeners and the speaker are tuned in for transmission.

As the candidate brings to the examination a book he has *enjoyed*, the examiner has the right to expect that the listening group will receive a series of experienced thoughts and not a succession of words. Questions may precede or follow the reading; it rarely happens that they are unfruitful.

Where there has been imaginative teaching the questions spark off perceptive comment. One boy who had seen and heard his book on both television and radio made a profound observation on the radio version: "It *looked* better." A fifth-former taking an advanced Senior Grade examination, who brought *Crime and Punishment* as her chosen book, was asked: "If you were dramatising this novel what would you want on the stage for your main 'set'?" In reply she said:

I did actually see Crime and Punishment done by the Polish company quite splendidly; I also saw the John Gielgud one which to my mind missed a good deal of the atmosphere of the book. I should want to have an abstract composite set like the Polish one, with no definite places on the stage. The English one was limited to three rooms and, therefore, Raskolnikoff's wandering through the city, so important in the book, was missed. With the abstract spacious set we could make the stage whatever our imaginations wanted it to be.

It is true, of course, that this girl is privileged both in her home background and in her school. She is fortunate to be taught by a teacher of English and another of speech and drama who open the shutters of the G.C.E. "O" level literature syllabus and let in the light. And there are many schools, but not nearly enough of them, where poetry, drama and the novel are living experiences and not school tasks.

In specifying a book which has been enjoyed we throw the net wide open; it is not unusual in a day's examining to have twenty-five different books. On the other hand, if a few of the candidates have chosen the same book, a whole episode can be covered with the group as one unit. It is an interesting test of communication and comprehension after the reading to reverse the order of speakers in a re-telling in their own words.

It would be misleading to suggest that all candidates presented for E.S.B. examinations are competent readers, for reading standards all over the country are not high, but in these assessments the teachers are present, and very often through the test they get a new perspective on their pupils. The successive years (and there are now a considerable number of boys and girls who have had an E.S.B. assessment for 5–10 years) usually show a steady growth in the quality of the work and the consequent enrichment of the personality.

Where spoken English is both taught and assessed, and reading aloud is a usual practice at every stage in school life, there are high standards of reading, speaking and listening. The by-products of this gradual training are many, since it subscribes in no small measure to social poise and personal relationships.

Reading aloud with a listening group is self-testing, for the group reveals at once whether its attention is held. If the reader who has failed to make her point is asked to question the listeners on the passage which has been read, she is usually quick to see that it is she who has failed if her listeners do not know the answers. Transmission has broken down.

Transmission is what matters. The examiner has a responsibility in this respect and over the years acquires various techniques to help various situations. Many of the weak readers have to be guided to constructive self-criticism or bolstered up so that they overcome inhibitions and fears and project their thoughts securely. As E.S.B. assessments are designed to teach both candidates and teachers, we go far beyond mere marking.

If, for example, the candidate has just made "print audible", a leading question often produces a self-analysis which hurts no one and profits the speaker. For example, the examiner might say: "If you wanted us to act that little scene after your reading, would you have read it any differently?" This draws various replies which usually pin-point the speaker's weaknesses: "Oh yes, I should have tried to make the conversation sound real," or "I'd have tried to make it more exciting," or "Yes, when he accuses him I'd have made it slower and more deliberate".

Sometimes the examiner may give the candidate a chance to try this out on one vivid phrase from the dialogue. The speaker dares then to enlarge the volume and range and is justly rewarded with attention from the listeners. This is no small conquest; it is a good step forward towards a newly found delight in personal communication.

When the candidate is asked to make these observations he can only do so in a buoyant atmosphere; there is no question of the examiner deflating him. Similarly there is a spontaneous check on the aural comprehension of the speaker and the listeners in the cross-questioning which may take place. The listening group has a positive function; it is not there to witness the exposure of weaknesses but to receive the message.

An experienced examiner gives an "impression" mark usually on a five-point scale which is based on the hearing of numerous candidates in numerous schools. Although it is an impression mark it includes conscious and subconscious evaluation of contributory factors:

1. Was the content understood?
2. Was the right atmosphere created?

3. Was the listening group arrested at once?
4. Was their attention held?

If there was partial or complete failure in 1–4, what were the causes?

(a) A lack of projection (diminished energy?—lack of confidence?—lack of practice?—physical limitation?—or lack of desire to "give"?).

(b) Limp physical stance—talking back to the book—sagging knees (was it lack of confidence?—lack of interest?).

(c) Limited vocal range—keeping to the middle flat notes of the speech register (lack of confidence?—lack of practice?—or limited imagination?).

(d) Limited flexibility of pace (lack of intelligence?—difficulty with mechanics of reading?—lack of imaginative awareness?— lack of oral practice?).

(e) Little use of pause (nervous tension?—lack of social rapport? —limited imagination?—or lack of skill in phrasing?).

(f) Weakness of articulation—physical flabbiness of muscles (social insecurity?—poor models for him to copy?—laziness or lack of interest?—regional weakness?).

(g) Muscular tension cramping vowels and voice (established habit from imitation?—psychological tension?—lack of security? —lack of social rapport?—lack of desire to communicate— reason?).

(h) Inaccurate pronunciation (unfamiliarity with words?— recognised accurately but never "voiced"?—lack of visual co-ordination?—imitation of poor model?).

One could elaborate endlessly on all the factors involved. Speaking at all is infinitely complex, reading aloud is even more so.

In the assessment for the E.S.B. the good examiner will not only decide the correct category in the A B C D E grade (or equivalent number grade), this is the least difficult task; he will comment on what is good and encourage the candidate to further effort. An insecure reader must not be dismissed with a "Weak" but rather he should have a constructive comment:

e.g. You could have a good voice. Open it out freely and imaginatively so that the listeners catch every point of the story. Try to practise every day.

Remember that most poor speakers and poor readers *are* poor because they feel that they are not worth listening to. The most meticulous day-to-day encouragement and help is needed. The smallest achievement must be noted and used as a rung for the next move up. Progress depends on success.

It is frequently argued that reading aloud has no place in modern life. We might stop to consider the good effects there might be if it had. It is true that many of the children we are now teaching have never been read to at home and have been deprived even in their schools of lively interpretation of books. Can we not ensure a better deal for *their* children? Every mother, father, elder brother and sister should be capable of reading to young children and to one another well. There is nothing which makes a closer family bond. On the more utilitarian level, reports, minutes, newspaper accounts, letters from friends and relations are part and parcel of the ordinary day-to-day reading aloud. It has been fashionable to reject it in education for too long.

High standards of reading aloud would lead to;

(a) literature being made more memorable through the triple impact of seeing, speaking and hearing;
(b) more aesthetic appreciation of style and content of literature which in turn would lead to a heightening of the sensibility of the reader;
(c) greater understanding of human character through identification with the experiences and talk of others;
(d) much more personal *enjoyment* of poetry, drama, novels, etc.;
(e) rhythmic sense of word values which not only makes print come alive but which affects the rhythm of the reader's personal speech;
(f) true understanding of tempo and pace which is implicit in good reading aloud—this gives the sense of selection;
(g) the heightening of key words and key phrases which is the basis of the ability to understand and to "précis";
(h) improved standards in the reader's personal articulation, vocal tone, vocal range and pace in ordinary conversation.

How to Arrive at an Assessment

As was said in the previous chapter, although one is giving an impression mark it is as well when making any judgements on oral work to assume, in the first place, if one is working on a five-point scale, that the speaker is of average ability until he proves otherwise —say C grade. In the case of reading aloud this should mean that: (a) he understands the passage, (b) he can be heard, (c) the voice can respond to the phrasing. When there is any weakness of deviation from that modest assumption the measuring needle swings over to D, or in extreme weakness to E. Similarly, if the audience is held, the atmosphere and style of the book communicated, the needle swings towards the B category. An A would only be given if the characterisation were colourful, dialogue spontaneous and communication with the audience so secure that the passage is made memorable. This judgement can apply to any age, if the book from which the reading is taken is the candidate's *own choice*.

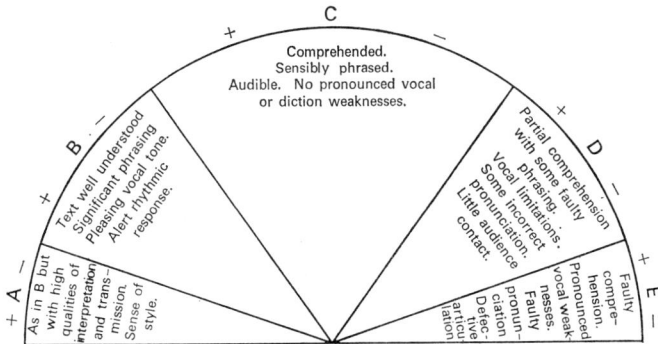

CHAPTER 5

Spoken Interpretation of Poetry, Prose or Drama

As WILL be seen from a close study of the syllabuses for the C.S.E. spoken English tests, none are including script-free oral interpretation except as a possible alternative. From discussion with members of English panels in general and C.S.E. panels in particular, one gets the impression that the majority of English teachers are suspicious of any inclusion of prepared work of poetry, prose or drama in a spoken English test. The arguments put forward are:

(a) that the candidate would rehearse his selected passage;
(b) that the teacher could impose an interpretation;
(c) that there would be an undesirable test of memorising;
(d) that preparation of words other than the speaker's own might encourage "elocuting" or "unnatural" speech;
(e) that the modern child has no practical use for such an exercise.

Let us deal with the points in turn.

(a) *That the candidate would rehearse his selected passage.* The idea seems to be prevalent that a sight-reading of a poem or literary prose is more "natural" and spontaneous than a prepared speaking. Nothing can be further from the truth. The best of the recordings of spoken verse, prose or drama are the result of the most meticulous study and repeated trials, rejections and selections. The more spontaneous the interpretation seems to be, the deeper will have been the investigation into the writer's meaning. A professional speaker experiments over and over again in order to get the perfection of cadence and rhythm which will do the best service to the writer's words. When the poet himself speaks the verse, apparently quite casually, he has in fact lived with his imagery and verbal cadences for a long time. It is certainly not a "sight-reading". He knows by now just where the pulsation of sound and silence is contributing to the meaning. Therefore we who are speaking his verse must relive the experience imaginatively before we can restate his words. How can this be done *without* rehearsal? A poem, read aloud for the first time, by an insensitive reader, may not be a poem at all.

If a professional speaker or actor feels that preparation and rehearsal are necessary, should we not try to give our own pupils the same kind of humility? This is not to suggest that school boys or girls should be giving a professional performance, but that they should be enjoying a truly creative experience. In a song, the notation, rhythm, tone and tone colour are prescribed, so the margin of error is narrower than in the interpretation of a poem, yet no one suggests that a song is ready, either to be enjoyed or heard, on a first reading.

(b) *That the teacher could impose an interpretation.* A good teacher of English will not "impose" but, with excellent material at his disposal, he will "inspire". If we are afraid of the teacher's influence, then we have appointed the wrong teachers. Those who have a genuine affection for literature and their pupils, and are on imaginative speaking terms with both, will, in any case, be worth imitating.

English teachers are fortunate in having, through their subject-matter, an opportunity to give their pupils a vision of excellence. They hold all the aces in their hands. Consequently, the good teacher of English makes every poem, story and drama "here today"; and because it is so, the boys and girls have a store of remembered literature for all their tomorrows.

(c) *That there would be an undesirable test of memorising.* The rejection of memorising is an understandable reaction away from the unimaginative exercise of "repetition". It was right that this should go. But the power of memory is almost limitless, provided it is *used*; and it is at its best in our school years.

If memorising of words grows from imaginative sensory experience, then it will make a path in the mind for further perceptive experience. The more we commit to memory, the easier it is to memorise. An actor who has experienced the emotions and reasoning of Macbeth, and memorised the lines, will not find it difficult to do the same with

Hamlet. But if in childhood one never had the habit or the enjoyment of knowing rhymes, stories and songs off by heart it may well be a considerable task for one to learn anything by heart in adolescence.

Of course one can understand the reaction against the sapless business of "learning by heart" when it was a device to ensure that pupils had neat slabs of quotable extracts for the English Literature paper; but this was merely "learning by rote"; since "heart" was the very quality which was missing.

Our own vocabulary experience is necessarily limited by our personal experience and personal acquaintance. Therefore, if we can get "language on the lips" of those who think and write more perceptively than we do ourselves, our horizons are widened and we are enriched. In any case the memorising is not an end in itself, it is usually the unsought bonus which comes from uniting imaginative impulse and the muscular activity of voice and speech.

Language rarely becomes our own through silent reading. Before we have confidence to use a word we must not only hear it but we must *say* it in its true context. The only way we can do this is through familiarising ourselves with the rich-textured language of others. The operative word is "familiarising", and this means making our "recognition" vocabulary into a "producible" one in oral practice.

(d) *That preparation of words other than the speaker's own might encourage "elocuting" or "unnatural" speech.* Another prevalent idea among teachers of English is that any speaking of words in a formal setting will result in "elocuting" or "unnatural" speech.

We have a different approach to French. We instal expensive language laboratories so that children can repeat over and over again the pure sounds, significant rhythm and intonation of a carefully selected and recorded master tape.

It is as well to remember that no speech is natural. "Back-street Salford" is no more natural than "Chelsea drawing room". All speech, whether it is in our own language or that of another country, is *acquired*. If the teaching of verse-speaking and drama results in what we derisively call "elocuting" then again we have appointed the wrong teachers. The good teacher will foster all that is best in the child's regional and family speech and in so doing will heighten sensibility to word values and their significant enunciation. But a democratic teacher—and surely all teachers should be that—will not want any child in his care to be limited by his family or street vernacular. If we can give the child experience of speech in many registers, then we are not only extending his oral powers; we are extending the child himself.

As Margaret MacMillan proved in her work for nursery schools, back-street speech limited children to back-street thinking and experience.

(e) *That the modern child has no practical use for such an exercise.* In education today we are all concerned that the curriculum should be sharply relevant to the life and environment of the pupils. This is commendable. But if we only teach that which can be *used*, we are giving education a very narrow definition. Through literature we can widen our experience and extend our environment. Because modern life has become for most people a mechanised materialistic business, is it not all the more important for us to give our young people human understanding through literature? There has been too little in our lessons "felt in the blood and felt along the heart". Through literature we can help to create young people who have the simple but profound quality of "caring". Only through dwelling on words which the writer has chosen, not just for their sense but for their *sound* and *rhythm* can one ever truly adopt them. As it is with people so it is with good writing, to enjoy either one must be on speaking terms.

But to be on speaking terms with language means that the words must not just be experienced in the mind but in the *muscles*. Education for aesthetic response can be cruelly handicapped when there has been no education in bodily movement.

If the muscles of the voice and speech mechanism have not been trained to respond significantly to language, what aesthetic response to literature can there be? As Margaret MacMillan points out in her educational treatise on the Nursery School: "Musicians, painters, instrumentalists, sculptors know that there is no creativity except through the most precise and significant motor control." Therefore, not only must our pupils hear literature spoken well, they must speak it well themselves, and enjoy the total physical and mental experience which the heightened language of poetry and drama can give. And if the language of literature is to become theirs—and this is a rich

4

gift we can give the poorest child—they must also be given the speech and vocal powers which can make this extended language a personal possession.

If we omit interpretative spoken English from our school assessments, who will take care of it?

Verse Speaking in the Context of a Spoken English Assessment

Obviously young people will be reading more poetry than they will be speaking, but if they themselves can speak a few poems *well*, and each member of the class speaks other poems well, the spoken anthology of the whole class is going to be a considerable one. If high standards are set by the teacher, professional recordings, and the children themselves in the studied poems, then eventually imaginative *silent* reading of poetry will not be outside the pupil's experience.

An immediate incentive for this kind of concentrated attention to poetry is to include verse speaking in the spoken English assessment. If, on "the day", twenty or so different poems have been heard significantly spoken, they will remain in the memory of the listeners and enrich their experience.

And how do some teachers produce poetry speaking which has significant intonation and a compulsive rhythm—poetry which really leaves the ground? And what has happened in teaching when a "dead-pan" face goes through the tortures of metric mumbling?

It is outside the scope of this book to give methods of teaching poetry; in any case it is usually a very individual affair which the teacher evolves for himself. In examining one hears the *results*, and one knows, from the moment a candidate says the first line, the quality of the teaching behind it.

No one can speak a poem well which he does not enjoy, so there should be no pressure about the choice of material. The teacher should see that the boys and girls have access to a wide range of poetry, perhaps in the first place, for those who seem resistant, verse with a contemporary appeal.

Success in verse-speaking, as in other sections of the exam, is success in *communication*. The poet's message must get across and the speaker must be the means whereby this happens. But he must not get in the way of direct transmission. Examiners, like all good listeners, are looking for interpretations of sincerity, sensibility and spontaneity. If a speaker is sincere there will be no preoccupation with the effect that he is making. He will be immersed in the imaginative experience of the poem. Even if there is vocal and technical limitation the quality of sincerity will still show through in the unforced rhythm and the expression in the eye.

Even the bluntest of children can be trained in sensibility; but it should mean what it says: a training of the senses which will lead to a heightened awareness and imaginative response. I do not believe that there are any children who are immune to the influence of poetry if it is introduced to them in the right way. But there must be a tingling of the senses and no evasion of, or embarrassment about, the emotional content.

I have heard tough boys in a condemned building in the heart of a northern industrial town speaking verse which would quicken the pulse of any listener. Yet if there had not been a spoken English examination which included this exercise they would never have reached this point of script-free imaginative interpretation. Indeed they might never have read poetry at all. We heard during a pilot C.S.E. examination a girl in an Essex secondary modern school speak the whole of Hopkins' "Leaden Echo"—her own choice—in such a way that an observing English master sitting just behind the examiner was heard to mutter: "I never knew what this poem meant until now." In the same examination a boy made us experience all the sensuous reaction of Wordsworth in the skating episode in the "Prelude". It was spoken with compelling verbal dynamism. Another boy who for years had dismissed poetry as "soppy" took us through Stanley Snaith's "Parachute" with a breath-taking recapturing of the experience. Careful study had produced spontaneity.

But in some of the C.S.E. pilot examinations which we held using the E.S.B. pattern, there were occasions when we almost regretted that we had included any memorised work. Many of the poems were merely "print made audible". Metre was often beaten out relentlessly and true rhythm was the first casualty. Too often there was no imaginative awareness so that the voice never ranged beyond the flat notes of the middle register. We experienced, too, in a few girls' schools, over-careful delivery which killed the rhythm, where the teacher had insisted "that every vowel had its full value" and "that every word must be finished off before starting another". At the other extreme we heard the casual perfunctory interpretation which ignored the stanzaic form and reduced the verse to prose. In a sense, all these speakers were *deprived* children, though they no doubt came from comfortable homes, and were being taught in expensively equipped schools.

How Are We to Judge the Speaking of Verse in the Group Assessment Situation?

First we must recognise that, for those to whom this is an unfamiliar experience, nervous tension may tighten the voice, restrict the tone and fetter the rhythm. The candidate, therefore, may not on this occasion produce the rendering which he may have evolved in his imagination or spoken on previous occasions. In his anxiety to get through without a lapse of memory he may also revert to a mechanical, rather quick tempo because he has no confidence to hold the pauses and make visual and oral contact with his listeners. It is the first duty of the examiner to create a climate in which the speaker feels at ease in giving voice to his imaginative thoughts.

Throughout the day, in the group assessments, the examiner will create an atmosphere of pleasurable expectation both for speakers and listeners. Instead of moving on from one item to another with the bare signals of: "Thank you" or "Now may I hear your poem?" or as one board practises, "Yes" or "Don't wait" or "Go on", he will show interest in the speaker's selection and add a comment which conditions him to the idea that there is to be reciprocal enjoyment. A possible approach might be: "Margaret, I see you've chosen Robert Frost's 'The Road not taken'. It's a favourite of mine. Have *you* ever had to make a decision in your life choosing between two possible directions? And, like Robert Frost, has it made all the difference?" Margaret then has a chance to talk easily and freely on some autobiographical experience and she can then move into the poem in continuing communication. If she sees no such parallel in her own life there could be an exchange of ideas on this situation arising in the future in choice of career or college, etc.

If the *teaching* of the poem grows in this way from personal emotional response to a shared experience, the nervous sensitivity will be creatively directed to the perceptive quickening necessary for the re-creation of the poem. John Dewey's precept on learning in general applies most pertinently in the experience of poetry: "in so taking hold of it (the poem) that he seems to have created it".

Sometimes there is a link between the poem and the book chosen for reading aloud. "I think, Peter, you must feel strongly about caged animals. You've chosen Cecil Day Lewis' poem 'Circus Lion' and the novel *Born Free*. Could you tell us first of *your* experiences and thoughts when you've seen caged or performing animals?"

Sometimes there is a link with a friend's choice of poem which has already been spoken: "Dick, I see you've chosen this fine poem of Wilfred Owen's 'Anthem for Doomed Youth' and John chose Siegfried Sassoon's 'Everyone Sang'. Do you know of any connection between the poems?" John may make his comment before Dick says his "Anthem for Doomed Youth". By this time the listeners also will be "there" in period and mood.

On a bleak November day in a classroom it may not be easy for Jennie to produce the warmth and ecstacy needed for, say, Laurie Lee's "April Rise" unless she has already been listening in a buoyant atmosphere. The examiner's attitude to the previous speakers, to the listening group and now to Jennie in particular will ensure that she does not have to make a "cold start". A warm smile, some appreciative comment such as: "What a splendid poem you've chosen, Jennie! Have you read Laurie Lee's 'Cider with Rosie'?" If she has not, then there is no suggestion that the examiner is doubting and questioning her background reading, but rather: "Well, that's a treat in store for you." If she has read it, there can be an agreeable exchange of shared delights which can include the listeners' comments.

If the candidate shows signs of tension before speaking, a shared joke, a friendly use of his name in a kindly exchange of small talk can help to put him at ease, though it is the experience of the English Speaking Board examiners that as soon as the day is in progress the nervous apprehension preceding the examination dissolves away. Where this kind of oral assessment has become a regular feature in the school programme there is no self-consciousness about the speaking of poetry or acting of drama before a responsive audience.

In his book *Examining Oral English in Schools*, Dr. Hitchman wisely suggests: "a short period of rest and silence is particularly necessary before the speaking of poetry in order to allow the candidate time to soak himself in the passage of verse and re-create the aesthetic apprehension that moved him in the period of preparation." Dr. Hitchman is talking there of the isolated candidate in the presence of an examiner. In the group situation it is a rather different matter; the atmosphere for the poem must be created for the *listeners* as well as the speaker. It is sometimes a help to let the candidate introduce his poem and perhaps also say why it has a special appeal, but sometimes a word from the examiner can put both the speaker and the listeners into the appropriate mood for transmitting and receiving heightened thoughts.

As in the other items in the spoken English test, the examiner should watch and listen generously, paying attention to the fine shades of meaning communicated through the *eye* as well as the voice. It is, therefore, unwise and unfair after hearing the title or the first line to start writing adverse criticisms. If the examiner is busy writing phonetic symbols of vowels which have gone rather wide of the mark in terms of "received pronunciation" he may completely miss the important truth that this Cumberland boy and Devonshire girl do know what they are talking about when they say: "It's a warm wind the west wind full of birds' cries." Although an experienced examiner may know that he has the expertise to be writing one thing and listening to another at the same time, the candidate does not. Suppose the speaker has been jolted into a new area of compassion in learning, for example, Raymond Tong's "African Beggar", he is going to be rather let down if his chief listener, the examiner, is looking critical, or is writing comments when he, the speaker, is endeavouring to transport his listeners to "the dust outside the Syrian store".

It is a deliberate strategy in the English Speaking Board examinations that the examiner is positioned slightly out of the direct focus of the speaker who then communicates with a genuine listening group. This also leaves the examiner more free to write during the actual speaking, but if he is wise this will not happen until he has given the speaker a fair hearing.

Although, as in the other sections of the examination, the examiner will give an "impression" mark, it will contain within it an evaluation of many factors which could roughly be grouped under the headings of (1) sincerity, (2) sensibility, (3) spontaneity. In some way, consciously or subconsciously, the examiner is being guided by some or all of the following considerations.

1. *Sincerity*
   (a) Is the speaker relaxed and "true" in stance and general attitude?
   (b) Has he made a genuine effort to get to the heart of the matter?
   (c) Is he communicating what he understands in a direct, unaffected way?
   (d) Has he made the poem part of his own experience?

2. *Sensibility*
   (a) Does the speaker respond to the sensory perception and imagery in the poem?
   (b) Has he made this part of his own imaginative experience?
   (c) Has he tuned in to the poet's choice of language and the "texture" of the words?
   (d) Is he able to convey this in his voice and speech?
   (e) Is he tuned in emotionally to the poet's experience?
   (f) Can he convey this through the tone and tone-colour of his voice?

3. *Spontaneity*
   (a) Has the speaker so taken hold of the words that he seems to have created them?
   (b) Is he re-creating the poem *now* for his listeners?
   (c) Can he tune in to the poet's compulsive rhythm which overrides but acknowledges the structural metre?
   (d) Can he speak whole thoughts so that they seem completely natural utterance yet are never in conflict with the stanzaic form?

Put into this tabulated sequence with every reaction accounted for, this all may seem too rarified and too demanding, and the teacher of English who has managed to get a few toughs to shed a little of their resistance to poetry by way of H. Webster's "Street Gang" or Charles

Causley's "Cowboy Song" may raise a questioning brow. But in some degree, whatever the poem and whoever the speaker, these factors still hold good. One can know, for example, a great deal about the qualities of an infant school teacher from the way her children speak something as apparently simple as: "I had a little nut tree."

A poem well spoken may take only 60 seconds to say, but if it is spoken well a lifetime of imaginative reaction will have gone into it and a lifetime of enrichment lies ahead.

Finally, a restatement of what has already been suggested earlier in this chapter is necessary. An examiner must not be preoccupied with "accent" or deviation from standard pronunciation. Of course he will be aware of it and should have a good enough ear and technical knowledge to be able to differentiate between honest sounds and slovenly speech. He cannot help but notice the intrusive R's, the glottal stops, the nasalised vowels, the spread S sound and the rest, but though his outward ear may be receiving these errors, his inward ear and eye will be making a broader, wiser judgement of the speaker's imaginative response to the poem. The examiner's written comments should deal in the first place with the success or failure in interpretation and communication. Where a written report is given, errors, weaknesses in voice or speech are put clearly in the *margin* as a guide for future work, or in a note at the end of the report. The main comment should be on the interpretation and communication of the poem.

Mark Assessment

As in the other sections of the assessment it is a good idea to assume an average mark until the speaker proves otherwise. Almost subconsciously the mental pointer hovers at the centre of the wide C division. Here for an average performance one should be able to take for granted the following basic factors:

(a) that the poem is understood;
(b) that the language follows the poet's order;
(c) that the rendering is audible;
(d) that the phrasing is not in conflict with the sense.

If there are breaks in the sense-phrasing or a mechanical metre asserts itself the magnetic needle will move towards D. If there is no true understanding of the poem and no true communication—and this will be rare—then the needle will move to E.

Conversely, is there is subtlety of intonation and inflection and flexibility in the rhythm with spontaneous changes of pace, pressure and pause which illuminate the meaning, the needle will move into the B grade. When there is heightened sensibility making the poem a complete personal experience and the voice and speech are such that the subtleties of the poet's imagery and music are truly communicated —and this will be fairly rare—the needle will move up to the A or distinction mark.

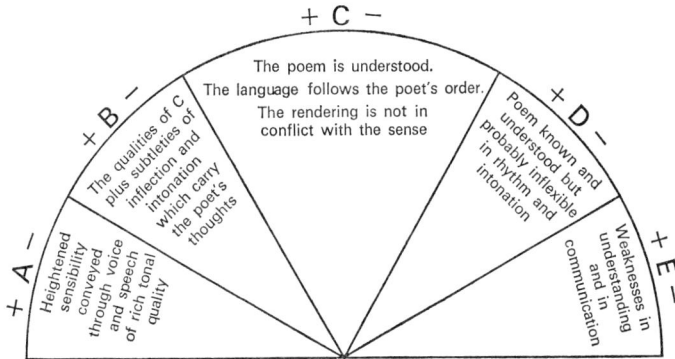

Of course, there will be other influences and other factors all modifying and manipulating the final marking position. The examiner of experience arrives at this apparently intuitively from the hundreds or thousands of speakers he has already judged. He knows the limitations and the potential of similar candidates of similar background; for somewhere he has heard perfection and failure—and hundreds in between. That experience establishes objective judgement, but in this work he is also dealing with a highly subjective art. His assessments must, therefore, always show the right kind of *subjectivity*.

Sometimes, for example, a speaker with a highly intellectual imaginative mind may have vocal or speech weaknesses which limit his communicative powers. The examiner in his remarks will indicate the A quality of the imaginative approach but may show that the delivery is only at C standard. The candidate and his teacher will then understand the B grading of a gifted and ardent student.

We should constantly remember that what is being tested is *communication*, but we must be on our guard not to give credit to the communicator who successfully communicates incorrect, inadequate or insensitive ideas!

To sum up on the assessment of verse-speaking, it is not a question of whether Jane Smith can put *herself* across, but whether she can bring the listeners into the poet's orbit, for it must be through her "awareness" that the listeners see through the poet's eye and hear through the poet's ear.

Drama as an Examinable Subject

In *Examination Bulletin* No. 1, issued by the Secondary Schools Examinations Council (H.M.S.O., 1963), the section on "Drama" began:

> In recent years drama has come to play an increasing part in the curriculum in secondary schools. The work has gone far beyond the conventional play production and provides a medium for pupils to express themselves creatively in speech and movement. Since this work is at an early stage of development and is highly individual, it is debatable whether it is a suitable subject for examination for the Certificate of Secondary Education.

My own opinion would be that, even with all the difficulties, it is well worth trying. Already in the E.S.B. exams, drama in small groups is an alternative choice to the poetry or prose in all the spoken English tests. I think we could go much further. It is easy to put forward many arguments *against* examining drama since most of the educational value is immeasurable. However, we all know that if a subject is not given the prestige status of an examination it tends to become edged out of the regular curriculum. When this happens, drama too often becomes the after-school activity for the enthusiastic, the talented or the exhibitionists. The inhibited, apathetic, ill-adjusted or those with an abundance of misused energy thus miss the very activity which they most need. When creative drama is omitted from the curriculum, too, the average child is denied the opportunity which creative drama gives him of finding new delights in living to the full stretch of his physical and imaginative powers.

If, however, we do include drama either as a part of the spoken English test or as a subject in its own right, we must be clear from the start about our objectives. We must not judge children on techniques which would belong more properly to a repertory actor on the proscenium stage, but rather consider how far the child has travelled through the experience of creative drama to a personal imaginative awareness. This presupposes that the class is being directed by a teacher who not only has heightened perception himself but whose whole attitude to education and the individual child is based on a sound philosophy.

Properly experienced drama should be the means whereby we learn:

1. To come to terms with varying personalities.
2. To recognise their conflicts.
3. To accept their differences.
4. To develop imaginative awareness in relation to other people.
5. To come to terms with language.
6. To extend our own linguistic powers through the rich experience and writing of others.
7. To develop the instrument of voice and speech for the communication of thoughts and emotions.
8. To develop response and co-ordination of the body and mind.
9. To release inhibiting tensions and direct muscular energy into creative channels.
10. To develop the personality to its full potential.
11. To extend imaginative awareness to all experience.
12. To work with a group to the full strength of one's powers.
13. To lose oneself in a corporate exercise.
14. To be responsible, in scripted drama, to the author, producer and, in a public performance, the audience.
15. To be resourceful in the creation and handling of costumes, props and scenery, so that the hand and eye are constantly and critically at work.
16. To develop faithfulness in carrying out minute details which contribute to the total group experience.

The difficulty in examining the subject is that the child with little performing talent may be the one who has contributed most in terms of 12, 15 or 16; or a child who has appeared in performance as uncertain and tentative may be the one who has progressed astoundingly from a paralysing initial awkwardness. It is, therefore, supremely important that in teacher-controlled examinations (and, of course, the specialist examining boards, too) we choose examiners with the right sense of values. It would be dangerous, for example, to choose an examiner simply because he made a good job of producing the school plays, or because he was a shining star in the local amateur dramatic society or had come into teaching from a frustrated professional acting career. This is not to say that these teachers might not *also* have acquired the philosophy and special experience of educational drama. If they have, then they would indeed be most valuable since they would combine their dramatic enthusiasm and expertise with sound educational psychology.

Examiners should, for example, be fully aware of the damage that could be done if a child, just beginning to blossom in the freedom of the creative drama class, became paralysed with nervous tension in the examination situation. The ideal examiner would also be aware that it may be the over-confident talented extrovert who is causing the gentle child to give a diminished interpretation.

But if the drama classes *throughout the years* have burgeoned in the way they should, then these extreme cases would already have become adjusted. They would not then be concerned whether there were observers or not, for they would be so happy in their achievement that sharing it with others would be an added delight. The examination should be just another "red letter" day.

In planning the syllabus for a test in drama it is important to give freedom for "own choice" of material and to go far beyond the conventional scripted play. It would be a mistake, however, to *omit* the scripted play since it is through the sensibility and writing of experts that our horizons can be extended. It is important in any group examination to discourage the solo performance and, in the solo examinations and festivals, positively to forbid the solo speaker popping through dialogue taking the roles of two or more characters.

Here is a suggested outline for a syllabus for a group drama examination where it should be possible to assess each individual contributor.

The group chooses one item from Section A and one from Section B. Section C in the examination is compulsory for all candidates.

A. *Unscripted Drama*

The group may present either:

  (i) a previously worked out and rehearsed interpretation of a story or stories;

or (ii) a documentary theme (this may stem from geography, history or social studies, etc.) worked out in terms of mime and movement with word and/or sound patterns;

or (iii) a mime or movement scene previously rehearsed, devised to interpret a piece of music.

B. *Scripted Drama*

The group may present:

  (i) a prepared scene or scenes from a play or plays;

or (ii) an acted and spoken ballad or ballads;

or (iii) short scripted scenes written by the pupils and presented in couples or small groups.

(In an hour's examination of twelve candidates it would be expected that A and B should take not more than 15 minutes.)

C. *Improvisation*

The examiner will divide the group into threes or fours and give a theme to each small group for improvisation. (Five minutes' preparation time will be allowed for all the candidates. The performances should take about 3 minutes each.)

The time allotted for the total examination should be approximately the equivalent of 5 minutes per child. The ideal size of group would be about twelve children for an hour's session, but the time could be adjusted for a larger or smaller group. Thus a class of twenty-four children should be allowed 120 minutes. It would, however, be much more manageable for the examiner to have them in two groups of twelve.

After the test an examiner should have at least half an hour (for a group of twelve) in which to go through his notes and marks. During this time any comments on the candidates' course work, e.g. contributions of original writing, making of props, devising of plays or mimes, technical work for stage, play-reading sessions, puppet theatres, etc., could be discussed either with the candidates individually or with the teacher and accredited accordingly either in a separate mark or a combined one.

The individual marking sheet prepared for the examiner's use should not only give the candidate's name but the various roles he is playing in the items presented. If the players introduce themselves and one another before the scene starts, this also helps the examiner in securing identity. Schools should be encouraged, too, to present to the examiner (and in the case of English Speaking Board perhaps the other observers) a neatly printed and designed programme made by the candidates themselves. This suggests to the children that any performance involves both players and audience in many different kinds of courtesy.

As in the other sections of the assessment the examiner should assume an average mark (C) until the candidate proves otherwise. The average child, in the dramatic items, should be concentrating on the characterisation and the situation in hand and should not be drawing attention to himself either with external display or with a negative attitude. He would be expected to use his imagination so that his body and speech respond to his thoughts. The candidate awarded the highest grade (A) would appear to have created the characterisation and the dialogue (if scripted) and be wholly absorbed in an imaginative world. There should be a real awareness in every way to the whole situation and the other characters in the scene, and this awareness should be communicated visually and orally.

The examiner should try to be aware of the *endeavour* and should not fail a young candidate who lacks technical expertise. It would be inadvisable to fail a candidate in a school group activity without a discussion with the teacher for there may be possible reasons for the shortcomings that day (illness, emotional trouble, absence, etc.).

Laziness, selfishness, apathy or lack of co-operation should, of course, be censored, but an enthusiastic teacher, one would have thought, would have dealt with these problems long before the day of the exam.

Here then are the qualities which should be taken into account in an assessment of drama in schools or youth clubs:

(a) Enthusiasm.

(b) Endeavour.

(c) Imaginative concentration.

(d) Significance of movement.

(e) Significance of speech.

(f) Response to others.

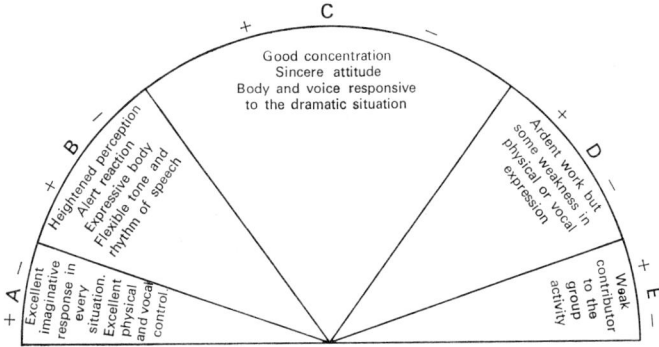

The candidate would be ungraded if through laziness, carelessness or apathy he failed to contribute to the group's dramatic message.

In marking candidates who are having some kind of professional training (e.g. Speech and Drama, College of Education, main or advanced course, B.Ed. degree course students) judgement must be stringent. In addition to the imaginative awareness the basic skills of acting, production and presentation must be mastered and put in practice. Styles of various types of plays must be truly understood and communicated through a well-trained body and voice.

CHAPTER 6

The Candidate in Active and Impromptu Communication

IN THE oral test for G.C.E. (London Board), Part II of this examination is a conversation between the candidate and the examiner. As in all other oral examinations the success of this depends almost entirely on the expertise and character of the examiner. In the conditions of this particular test, the candidate sits at the opposite side of the table in a private meeting with the examiner who then opens the conversation with some reference to the reading passage which the candidate has already read aloud in Part I. The examiner is advised that he is not concerned with checking comprehension, but is rather using this preliminary talk as a way in towards an acceptable talking point from which he hopes the candidate can take over.

There is therefore a certain hazard here as to whether the examiner will, within the time available, ever arrive at a subject where the candidate can be vitally informative. As we have pointed out in this book before, people cannot speak successfully and convincingly (and why should they?) unless they are at home with the subject and, ideally, at home with the listener or listeners. It would seem then that there could be an arbitrary quality about this type of conversation, but the most successful examiners of this Board no doubt develop a sixth sense which makes them able to make intuitive and imaginative conversational moves, and from the kind of response they get from the candidate they sense when to withdraw and let the candidate take over. It is asking for verbal deadlock if the examiner comes armed with a list of topics and propels a random choice on which the candidate must talk. How frustrating, for example, for the boy who has spent his summer vacation working in a *kibbutz*, and is not keen on water sports, to be asked to talk on "Sailing", or for the boy who has worked at the week-ends building a house-boat to talk on "Pop Groups", or for the girl who has taught herself braille in order to read and write letters for the blind to have to give an arid little commentary on "Bicycling". Yet if the *examiner* fails to get on the right wavelength he will be jeopardising the candidate's chance of success. On the other hand, it is reasonable to assume that a 16-year-old boy or girl should be able to talk on a variety of topics of general interest.

There is of course some justification for this type of exercise, since there will be several occasions when boys and girls will be interviewed by strangers who may be indifferent to their special interests, prowess, discoveries and beliefs. In this event, however, the interviews will have a specific purpose, and the conversation will be geared accordingly: e.g. entrance to college or university; consideration for a certain post or application for grant-aid, . . . Obviously the interviewer, in this case, has specific information he wants to draw out, and the manner in which this information is given will give him a good idea of the interviewee's temperament and personality.

The task of the examiner in the E.S.B. and certain C.S.E. spoken English tests, which include a personal project, is at once both simpler and more demanding. Throughout the prepared talk the examiner will be listening generously, but his experience will make him aware of any weakness in the argument, points which are not clear or which are worth amplifying. He may notice a stage in the project where a manual demonstration with a verbal commentary would clarify the exposition, free the talk from its structural rigidity and extend the speaker's range. The examiner is therefore ready to ask for this when the talk is over. For example, the boy who had given a clear but rather detached talk on the construction of a radio was asked how he would set about finding the fault in a radio brought to him for repair. The boy then asked for chalk, and with much more freedom and vitality than he had shown in the prepared talk, gave a verbal and blackboard explanation of the vulnerable parts of the radio, and how he would test them.

The skilled examiner never asks questions which bring monosyllabic answers or mere agreement, but always frames the questions

5

in such a way that the candidate has to consider and then take over in *continuing communication*. He becomes absorbed in the thinking process. In the early days of the English Speaking Board, when we were trying out potential examiners, an academically highly qualified and charming examiner smiled her way through this profitless conversation with a polite and patient 12-year-old.

"Do you like going for walks in the country, Jane?" . . . "Yes."

"Have you a dog?" . . . "Yes."

"Do you take him with you?" . . . "Yes."

"Does he enjoy it?" . . . "Yes."

"How old is he?" . . . "Seven."

"That makes him forty-nine in human years, doesn't it? Much older than you! How old are you?" . . . "Twelve."

The girl had preceded this vacuous part of her test with a diligent little talk on her own puppet theatre which she had brought with her. In conversation after the examination we discovered that she had made all the puppets herself including the papier-mâché heads. What a profitable 2 minutes the examiner and the audience could have had learning how to make the models, and how demanding this would be in testing the candidate's ability to inform, explain and instruct. In brief, an examiner must have a spirit of genuine enquiry, and the indefinable quality which Lancashire folk call "Nous" and Yorkshire folk call "Gumption".

On another occasion a more imaginative examiner asked a girl candidate, who had talked on the making of puppets, to put one on each hand and have a conversation between any two of the characters. As one puppet she chose was a witch and the other a rather defiant young girl, there was much scope for spirited improvisation.

In the group type of spoken English examination the questions do not need to be allocated to a special part of the test; they do, in fact, occur at any stage. The group themselves are often explosive with questions, and when they are not, the examiner can soon raise a point which evokes a speaking and listening response. The speaker then replies in a genuine desire to impart information to a group genuinely wanting to receive. For example, here is one examiner's question after a "pastry-making" project. "You said that it was important to keep the hands cool. Can you tell us precisely why, and demonstrate with your hands, while you explain, the method you use in combining the fat and the flour?"

Another examiner's question to a boy of 10 was: "You've given us excellent instruction on how you made your home-made kaleidoscope, Timothy. Now put it to your eye and describe the particular pattern which you see. Try to make *us* see it!"

On another occasion a 15-year-old boy with the project "The electric power of our town", was immediately questioned by his contemporaries: "Can you think of any way we could reduce the cost of electricity?" . . . "Do you think in the United Kingdom we could make more use of water power, especially the sea?" . . . "What would be the difficulties involved in using nuclear power for domestic purposes, and how far have we got in this country in bringing this about?"

The examiner's question was: "In doing this project you must have had to make many enquiries and write many letters. Can you tell me more about the personal contacts you made and how you got your information?" In discussion with staff we have discovered that where the candidate has gone beyond the school walls, in his quest for information, he has usually grown in enthusiasm, patience, knowledge, social poise and friendly response to adults.

Very often the examiner's request involves the audience in practical participation either in small groups or as a whole.

PROJECT: *Captaining the School Sailing Club*
After the talk the examiner said: "Will you choose your crew, bring them out here on to the boat and give them their various jobs? Get the boat out of a difficulty."

PROJECT: *Four Generations in the Potteries* (the girl's mother, grandmother and great-grandmother had all been pottery decorators and the girl herself wished to do the same)
The examiner asked at the conclusion of the talk: "Will you teach the group how to set out the pattern on the plate, and show the first process in the painting?" A further question was: "How do *you* judge what is good design and what is not?"

One of her colleagues enquired: "How many hours a day did your Grannie work?" It could have produced a monosyllabic answer, but in fact the girl at once made Grannie come alive for us as she flowed on from the opening words of: "My Gran says that. . . ." If on the other hand she had simply said, "Twelve", then the examiner could have shown her interest by asking to hear more of Grannie's experiences. But in this case a whole area of communication and a most worth-while strengthening of a personal family relationship had come about from the pursuit, by this girl, of this single project.

PROJECT: *Hazards of Pot-holing* (an 18-year-old technical college student in Cumberland)

After the talk two boys and two girls were invited to come out and discuss with him "Can discomfort bring happiness?" There were interesting contributions here; one was a climber, another a swimmer, the second boy a rugby player and the second girl a "sybarite", though she described herself more simply as "thoroughly nesh". Obviously she preferred comfort, and from her easy-going attitude in the group she was not fond, either, of verbal combat.

PROJECT: *The "Cathys" of our Town* (a study of the local housing conditions by a 16-year-old girl)

A spirited discussion followed the prepared talk between herself and two other girls whose projects respectively were to be: "The folly of early marriages" and "Population Explosion". Questions followed from the floor. At the end there was a little more appreciation of the local council's problem but stringent examination of public expenditure and personal responsibility.

PROJECT: *The Four-stroke Engine*

This talk, which was clarified with accompanying diagrams, evoked the following request from the examiner: "Would you tell us how to maintain a car engine and then answer the listeners' questions?"

PROJECT: *Some Post-Eliot Poets* (given by a sixth-form arts student in the presence of his science colleagues)

At the end of his prepared dissertation the examiner commented: "You said that contemporary poets deal with vital human experiences. Perhaps some of your friends here haven't much time for poetry, but all the same they, too, are vitally interested in human experience. Ask them about this now, and then recommend a poet or poems which you think they'd . . . I can't think of a better expression than your own here . . . *dig*."

Verbal interaction followed here with one or two possible converts.

PROJECT: *History of Tennis* (fifth-form grammar-school girl)

"Could you tell the listeners the difference between real tennis and lawn tennis?" After she had explained about the corruption of "royale" to "real", the indoor court, the smaller racquet, the different techniques and that Henry VIII played the game, she was asked to invite three of her friends out and teach them how to serve in lawn tennis. She did this in action and checked on her colleagues' mobile interpretation of her commands.

In the primary stages it is usually easy to break away from the child's set talk into more active and spontaneous communication. One can ask from genuine enquiry and often in real ignorance even at this stage: "When I was a little girl, Stella, none of us had hamsters for pets. Can you tell me when they first came to England and which is their native country?" If she does not know she is, of course, not penalised. The examiner might say cheerfully, "Does anyone else know?" If there is still uncertainty the examiner might add, "Well, that's something we can all try to find out, isn't it?" One examiner's "hamster" question followed a rather more unorthodox talk which included odd dietary details. She asked, "But how exactly did you discover that your hamster's favourite food was a slice of swiss roll with Oxo poured over it?"

After a live demonstration and talk on sweet-making another examiner said: "We enjoyed watching you make the sweets for your party, Sheila. Now pretend your guests are here, welcome them to your house and teach them a game that you are going to play."

"What a delightful collection of foreign dolls, Bridget. Will you pretend that your favourite one is lost and that you are asking the listeners to help you to find it. Describe it exactly and check that your listeners know all the facts so that they could recognise it."

"Shall we let your friends come round and have a closer look at your model you've made of your local station. Will you tell them exactly how you made the bridge and explain to them how the signals work." Questions are certainly not elementary in the primary school. On this particular occasion one 9-year-old boy asked the speaker to say why he thought this station should not be closed down as was threatened. All the class joined in its defence!

It is always a delight for an examiner to receive a completely unexpected answer. One E.S.B. examiner, having listened to and watched a very deft and definite demonstration by a 10-year-old boy on aircraft modelling, asked: "Some people might not be as successful as you are in making models. What are the most important qualities for a model-maker to have?" (no doubt expecting the answer: "patience" or "accuracy" or "neat fingers"). The reply was much more interesting: "Oh you don't need much, sir, intelligence and glue!"

Questions and Impromptu Talk Arising from the Reading

When each candidate brings a book he has enjoyed, it is not an unusual experience, as has already been said, for twenty-five different books to appear during the day. This evokes many opportunities for different kinds of communication which may include (a) recommendation, (b) exposition, (c) observation on characterisation, (d) comparison of the television, radio or film interpretations, etc.

One comment remembered with pleasure was a 14-year-old girl listener's spontaneous persuasion: "Oh go on, can't you tell us what happened next?" As so often in the group situation the audience is the reliable indicator of the speaker's success in communication. Often the examiner's question precedes the reading. For example, after a brief look at the cover an examiner might say to the audience: "Look, Richard's book won the Nobel Prize! Will you tell them, Richard, why you think it did?"

Similarly: "Will you explain to the audience, Roger, why the book is called *The Wooden Horse*?"

"It's twenty years since I read *Thirty-nine Steps* and I've forgotten the end. Will you remind me about it and tell the listeners if you think it is a satisfactory conclusion, Rachel?"

"Which do you think was the most agonising moment in . . . *Kon tiki* or *Silas Marner* or *Jane Eyre* or *Rebecca* or *The Ark* or *The Silver Sword*? Can you describe it as if it were happening *now* and that you were involved in the experience?"

"If you were to be cast in a play or a film of *Lord of the Flies* which boy would you like to be and why?"

"Here in front of you I want you to choose the four March girls. Will you also say, Angela, why you have chosen each one for the particular part and give your Amy, Jo, Meg or Beth any further information they may ask for?"

To a 17-year-old girl in a public school with a tradition of social service: "If you had lived in the 'Lark Rise to Candleford' period, what social service would you have wanted to do?" The girl who was asked this question said that she would have turned her manor house into a free school for all the children in the village.

After a very nervous girl of 14 had read her extract from "Heidi" in a way which did not do justice to her imagination and intelligence, I asked her to put her book down and without looking at it pretend that she was Heidi calling out a greeting to her grandfather who was just coming in at the door (an episode from her tensely read passage). It demanded a completely different voice and manner from the closed-in diffident pianissimo she had used for the reading. Mustering all her powers she moved towards the door and called out in a stronger more buoyant voice: "Hello Grandfather, I'm glad to see you!" and then the tears, which she had kept out of sight with real difficulty throughout the test, gushed out. Perhaps the reader would feel critical of an exam or an examiner which produced tears, but I knew that this small achievement brought relief, satisfaction and joy all in one, and that she would never have the same fears again in speaking before a group. This belief of mine was supported by an answer the girl gave in an anonymous questionnaire prepared later by the headmistress—but she could hardly remain anonymous to me—the questionnaire asked: "Which part of the spoken English test did you enjoy most?" To which she answered: "When I became Heidi and called out to my grandfather." Notice the very significant words "became" and "my". In identifying herself with Heidi she was able to move away from her own tense body into another image which liberated her.

Questions Arising from the Poems

One would never want to use a poem as a mere paraphrasing exercise, but often it is necessary for the speaker or reader to put some part of it into his own language to elucidate the poet's particular meaning and to reveal his own imaginative experience. This perceptive response will show orally—and aurally—through a certain intonation of a line, perhaps an unusual or significant stress, an incongruous or illuminating tone-colour. These can give rise to the examiner's enquiry and afford the speaker an opportunity to share or explain his particular interpretation.

If, for example, a child has spoken the modern sonnet "The Common Street" by Helen Gray Cone and given us the "pure splendour" of the sunset in the grey street in the completing sestet, we may just want to be silent in an appreciative glow or share our delight with some comment to the audience. We must not think that because it is an examination we must continually seek for information. But if, perhaps, the speaker has missed the contrast of the golden glow which follows the drab grey of the opening octave, he might be more successful in describing spontaneously a comparable experience of his own. One 13-year-old boy who failed to react to this poem gave me an impromptu commentary on the Blackpool illuminations which had both sparkle and glow. Perhaps "The Common Street" was not really his own choice but a prescription from his teacher—or maybe he was a likeable Philistine!

After an appreciative speaking of Philip Larkin's "At Grass" by a 15-year-old girl who was "crazy about horses", I asked her to slip back in time to when one of the old horses, described in the poem, knew "the starting gates, the crowds and cries" and she chose to tell of the excitement and feelings of the racehorse as if she herself were the horse "under starting orders".

In a brief conversation preceding a 16-year-old boy's speaking of "Sunday morning Kings Cambridge" by John Betjeman, we learned that he, too, had been a choir boy. After his competent and intelligent speaking of "Kings" he was asked to tell us about the midnight service on Christmas Eve in his own church. This account had the compulsive rhythm of immediacy which had just eluded him in the speaking of the poem, because of course, in this case, he, like the poet, was recording his own particular observation and experience, but without the experience of the poem or other poetry his own powers of description might not have developed to this stage.

Another boy spoke Robert Frost's "Out, out—" (the poem where the boy's hand is cut by the circular saw) with the kind of appalling truth which only the imaginative young can experience. He told me that he had had nightmares about it after reading it, but even so he felt he wanted to learn it. Perhaps, if nightmares are the penalty we pay for increased compassion for others, we should not try to protect our young even from that experience.

After a virile speaking of Michael Roberts' "La Meije 1937" in which we hear the description of Ottone Bron's fall to death while climbing a glacier, I asked the technical college student if he knew that Bron's motto was: "Always do the most difficult thing." Could he tell us of times when he himself had gained some satisfaction from doing something difficult? He said modestly that he had never done anything to compare with Bron's bravery but, diffidently at first, he began to tell, without a trace of sentimentality, certain difficulties in his life in trying to share and communicate all his experiences with parents who were both totally blind. Such occasions are salutary for listeners and examiners. Indeed as an adult observer said on another occasion: "We find we are examining ourselves."

The poem "Stanley Matthews" by Alan Ross is not as simple as the title might suggest. I, therefore, checked that the many allusions and non-English references—which seemed outside the range of a 15-year-old boy—were understood. Having done this I next learnt that the boy had seen Matthews play, and in a voice with an attractive northern tang, he added his own simple comment: "I think the Queen did right—to make him a Knight."

The examples given in this chapter picked out here and there from candidates geographically ranged from the north-east of Scotland to the south-west of England, academically ranged from the university scholarship winner to the factory day-release student, socially ranged from the upper-class public-school boarder to the Dr. Barnardo boarder in an industrial city school, and ranged in age from the primary school to the college of education, are not to show any definite method of oral questioning, nor should they be tried out by other examiners for they will not fit another occasion. They arose from the particular time and the particular candidate.

But perhaps they will serve to show that if we have a true examination of spoken English we must get through to the candidate and see and hear him *at the centre of his own thinking*. We must not put him through a series of prefabricated exercises designed to produce "instant talk".

Our aim must be "total communication" and to do this we must give the maximum amount of scope and stimulus within the necessarily limited time at our disposal.

CHAPTER 7

Spoken English Tests in the Certificate of Secondary Education

PERHAPS of all the subjects considered for examining in the Certificate of Secondary Education, it is the spoken English test which has caused the most trouble. Public examinations previously formulated and executed were based on the assumption that one was testing on a prescribed syllabus and/or an extended cumulative experience. Consequently written examinations developed in a traditional manner with cautious evolutionary rather than revolutionary changes.

Faced as we are with a new situation and a new challenge, there is little wonder that there has been much apprehension about validity, objectivity and reliability in the testing of spoken English for C.S.E. involving, as it does, huge numbers of our school population. But these are not the only things we must guard, for the examination which can be streamlined administratively and be most accurately marked, may have the least educational value. Subjects that are not so much concerned with the absorption and manipulation of facts and figures, but which test a child's creative, interpretative, aesthetic and kinaesthetic response defy completely objective analysis. Indeed, in these spheres, subjective judgement is demanded.

From the pilot and early tests carried out by the various C.S.E. Regional Boards and the careful wording of some of the syllabuses, one can deduce that much conferring produced the deceptively simple directives which occur in some form in practically every region. Most Boards, quite rightly, were concerned that this must not be a test of "elocution" nor an assessment of the candidate's proximity to "received pronunciation". Here are a few directives which make that clear:

(East Midland) "Local dialect will be acceptable but slovenly speech will be penalised."

(Yorkshire) "Local groups of teachers should be competent to decide how far local accent should be penalised."

(North West) "The moderator will not under any circumstances penalise a child for having a strong local accent."

(South East) "Regional variations in accent and dialect will be accepted provided that they do not interfere with the ability to communicate."

(South West) "Regional accents will be fully acceptable provided that they can be understood by persons not familiar with them."

(Middlesex) "It is not intended as an elocution test. Incoherent and indistinct speech will be penalised, but no candidate will be penalised because of accent."

(Metropolitan Region) "It is accepted that within the Metropolitan area are to be found wide differences in accent and speech habits largely due to social differences and to the presence of children from overseas. It is not intended that any candidate should be penalised because of his variation from an almost indefinable norm."

It seems advisable for all Boards to make some similar kind of statement relative to regional speech. The full explanation given by the Metropolitan Region is most pertinent but the same directive is needed for many urbanised areas: Liverpool, Birmingham, Leicester, Coventry, Corby, Scunthorpe, etc., where there has been extensive immigration not only from overseas but from other parts of the United Kingdom.

In addition to the directives on local speech, the stated criteria demonstrate liberal attitudes:

(Associated Lancashire Schools) "The general aim of the examination is to test the child's ability to express and transmit ideas and feelings to an audience through the spoken word. Assessment will have due regard to audibility, intelligibility and expressiveness."

(Metropolitan) "The purpose of the examination is to give the candidate an opportunity to demonstrate his powers of personal communication and his command of spoken English."

(East Anglia) "Teachers will have freedom to interpret the individual needs and interests of their pupils, and independent initiative and experiment will be welcome."

(Middlesex) ". . . to test the candidates' ability to communicate clearly and sensibly, in a lively manner, by means of the spoken word."

(South West) "This is intended to test candidates' ability to communicate facts, ideas and opinions, and to speak and read effectively. The test is mainly one of communication."

(North West) "(a) transmit ideas and feelings,
(b) describe what has been experienced,
(c) narrate,
(d) present and discuss a point of view."

(South East) "Subject matter, accuracy of expression, range of vocabulary and clarity and fluency of diction are the criteria for assessment both in the interview and by the school."

(North West) "(a) Audibility—can we easily hear what the candidate says from 15 or 20 feet away?
(b) Intelligibility—does the candidate understand what he is saying, does he involve himself successfully in his task so that by variations of pitch, pace, power and pause he is able to be understood?"

(Yorkshire) "The candidate will, in his oral work, be marked on his ability to express himself without confusion, his range of vocabulary and expression and his general maturity in the use of language as a means of communication."

(West Midlands) "The aim is to test the ability of candidates to communicate ideas, feelings and information in a clear and interesting manner. . . ."

(East Midlands) "The candidate should be able to communicate ideas, facts and feelings effectively by means of the spoken word."

(West Yorkshire and Lindsey) "The candidate will be expected to understand the spoken word and use it effectively" . . . "The test should give the candidate the opportunity to express his own thoughts as an individual and as a member of the group."

6

So far, so very good. The aims are commendable, but if we examine each syllabus in detail, there is evidence that in many cases a candidate may not have a real opportunity to live up to these aims. (See chart in folder.)

Let us consider these questions:

1. We are agreed that we are examining oral communication; can we define what this includes or should include?

(a) Communication of information?—if so, *whose* information? Surely the candidate's. If there is no preliminary study or investigation can the examiner ever hope to get informed communication?

(b) Communication of ideas?—one can only have worth-while ideas if one has grappled with genuine situations before the examination. If the project, prepared book, poem, prose or drama are the candidate's own choice, then one can expect him to communicate ideas sparked off by the examiner's and listeners' enquiries. There is no danger of this being pre-fabricated. The candidate will only have supplied, as it were, "the warp"; it will be the interaction of all the listeners controlled by the examiner which will create the threads into the final "weft".

(c) Communication of feelings? One cannot put feelings into words unless sensibility has been heightened and language extended through worth-while personal experiences or vicarious experience through literature. Are we not limiting the scope here if we exclude, as many Regional Boards do, any oral interpretation of literature or creative writing?

2. Who is to be in authority? Can one speak well if one is not? Obviously we should do all we can in an oral test to give the *candidate* a chance of being an authority. This can only be so if he is allowed to talk on some subject with which he has contended or practised enjoyably. If in addition the examiner is genuinely using the candidate *as a source of information*, then real conversation will flow.

3. Can the candidate give information freely and enjoyably if *his only listener* is on the official side of the table with all the trappings of mark sheets, stop-watch or worse still, tape-recorder? Would it not be more valid to have a group whose only function is to listen and respond?

4. Can a candidate communicate successfully to an examiner if there is a cultural barrier between them? It is important not only to engage wise, human, modest and stimulating examiners, but to have a group of listeners with whom the candidate is ON EQUAL TERMS.

5. As we can only talk well in response to the right kind of stimulus, is it not important to have oral exchange which stems from rich experience both inside and outside the school? Is it not implicit in such a test that all subjects and skills (e.g. handicrafts, cookery, science, etc., including the handling of the relevant gear) can be reckoned to be appropriate for the spoken English test? Would this not help to extend linguistic experience in class and outside school before, during and after the C.S.E. examination?

6. Language is a form of behaviour. Should we not, therefore, in an oral test (and "aural" is implicit here) take into account attitude, response, reaction and reciprocity? Is it not more valid to do this in relation to a *group*, since a single examiner might evoke particular and individual reaction?

7. Is there a danger in introducing a test which gives neglected children another situation in which they can fail? Have we any right to examine in the FINAL YEAR of school something as important as oral communication unless we have given systematic imaginative education in the subject—and assessed it—from the earliest school age? Does not the wording in some of the syllabuses suggest that there should be no previous training, rehearsal or preparation? Yet the linguistically deprived children (and these are a big percentage of our school population) need careful, personal and encouraging help at every stage in school life.

8. Are we in danger of creating another examination where the child with the recognised high I.Q. can score again? Should we not be creating an examination which can provide a meeting place in which we can listen to and reward every different kind of intelligence—the patient craftsman, the slow but sure "prober", the creator either with hands or imagination, the socially aware and responsive, the dependable artisan and the enthusiastic enquirer. All these people can share the fruits of their labours in the spoken English test and learn through this experience to appreciate one another.

Scope and Limitations of the C.S.E. Syllabuses in Spoken English

In the tables set out in the folded chart are the various elements of the C.S.E. regional panels' spoken English tests and, in brief terms, the particular method chosen for administration. In addition there are many variations on the same themes in the alternative "Modes" chosen by individual schools too numerous to tabulate here. Not one of these syllabuses was devised without considerable conference, or genuine concern that the test should be "child-centred", but too often the result is an uneasy compromise or a deliberate restriction in an effort to conform to a limited time, to be technically and aesthetically undemanding, to avoid any guided rehearsing, to rationalise and simplify the work of the examiner, and to streamline administration.

This was understandable when a wide-scale examination was being newly devised without a tradition of oral teaching or oral examining.

The National Association for the Teaching of English has summarised possible methods in its Criteria of Success in English and added its constructive criticism:

> As a start, three ways have been suggested for restricting the scope of the examination and thus temporarily simplifying the problem (see *Examination Bulletin* No. 1). The first is to test for *effective communication* between the candidate and a familiar audience, that is, a small group of fellow candidates and/or a teacher-examiner. This approach is a natural development of the sort of assessments that can be made throughout the course by a teacher working with his class. Thus over the year he can ensure that speech has been assessed under normal conditions and over a wide range of activities. At some convenient time one or more external examiners will visit the school to moderate a sample of assessments. This is the point where oral assessment is most time-consuming; if, for example, candidates are assessed individually it is unlikely that an examiner will moderate more than 25 in a day. Clearly, therefore, active participation by large groups of English teachers is essential to this mode of assessment and though we are well accustomed to impression marking of language in its written form, the need for all of us to learn new techniques, devise schemes, and agree on standards, calls for regular local and regional meetings (and appropriate work in teacher training).
>
> The second method is to test aural comprehension. The Birmingham Working Party suggest that, using written answers, an objective assessment is possible. We have some reservations. The danger of objective tests in aural English is that they become predictable and may encourage limited teaching. We note also that a conversation, interview, or question time after a prepared

talk all give scope for assessing aural comprehension, in each case with the certainty that the language to be understood is *spoken* English, not written English read aloud.

The third approach is to test *oral expression*. This implies not the traditional reading of a set passage, alone before a strange examiner, but an approximation to classroom conditions, the candidate being asked to give a prepared talk to a small group of his fellows, preferably on a subject that has arisen in the normal course of English work. The external examiner(s) will then assess the effectiveness of his presentation and delivery. Where poetry or prose is to be read aloud, there is a strong case for candidates making their own choice (with help where needed), and being given ample time to prepare and "rehearse" their reading.

We are all indebted to the members of the Southern Region panel who carried out a series of four separate tests followed by exhaustive and constructive reports in order to discover which *one* of the four methods could prove to be the most fruitful test.

METHOD 1. *Reading aloud*

The candidate was to select a book which he or she knew pretty well and liked. The examiner chose a passage and gave a moment or two for perusal. The reading was then used to initiate conversation (see comments in Chapter 4, Reading Aloud).

METHOD 2. *Prepared talk and discussion* arising from it with a group who could ask questions. (See Chapter 3, Personal Projects.)

METHOD 3. *Private conversation about a visual stimulus*

The candidates were presented with a diagram of a town which marked roads, shops, parks, schools, etc., which was followed with interrogation from the examiner and conversation.

METHOD 4. *Group discussion*

The candidates were given three of the topics half an hour before the test and others were introduced when the initial discussion began to falter.

Subjects: Hair styles, fashions in clothes, local affairs, leisure activity, television programmes, coffee bars, etc.

As Method 1 and Method 2 have been discussed in detail in Chapters 3 and 4 respectively, let us consider Methods 3 and 4—their advantages and disadvantages.

It is obvious from the Southern Region report that Method 3 was carried out with the interviewer/interviewee procedure. This seems to cut out the very obvious value of an oral assessment: that is the give and take and stimulus of a participating group. It would seem, and this is supported by the examiners' report, that the whole test could become far too much of a question-and-answer situation with the examiners necessarily dominating and initiating. One would think, too, that there are some young people who are especially intelligent about diagrams and symbols and others who are equally intelligent but need the response of a more human direct approach. If the speaker's attention is focused down on to such a small visual area might there not be a resultant tension and inhibition? This would mean that there could be little evaluation in the test of projection and audience contact and the repeated exercise could become extremely tedious for an examiner. On the other hand, such a chart could be a means whereby the examiner could find an acceptable talking point from which the candidate could then take over.

Method 4, the group discussion, we feel is an excellent idea if it is based on something which has had previous considered thought or direct personal investigation and experience. However, we found in the E.S.B. pilot scheme tests for C.S.E. that when subjects such as Hair Styles, Pop Music or Fashions are introduced the candidates use their vocabulary in its most feeble form. After all, the extended vocabulary for such subjects depends on a professional expertise and narrowly registered jargon—and an echo of the appropriate jargon might very well belong to the glib little reader of women's magazines.

It would seem to be a grave mistake to judge a child's communication on the single item of free conversation on a topic suggested by the candidate which may be of only temporary or fleeting interest. If the candidate feels that he is to be awarded 20 per cent of the total English marks on superficial chatter then both examiners and candidates will be subscribing to a lowering of standards and the challenge and opportunity of an exacting and exciting spoken English test will be lost.

Let me give an example of a recent experience in a northern industrial town. It had been suggested that during a week-end training course for teachers on the teaching and examining of spoken English, the two E.S.B. exponents should conduct a small demonstration examination. The four candidates who were presented had been prepared not on an E.S.B. formula but what seemed to be, on first reading, a worth-while C.S.E. syllabus. Each had prepared a talk—

this turned out to be a written essay which never left the hand—and they each brought a book they had previously read.

An attractive, healthy, clear-skinned 15-year-old had chosen as her subject "Twiggy" (to the uninitiated let me explain that Twiggy in 1967 was the leanest and lankiest of "models" who made a fortune modelling "kooky" clothes. No doubt by now Twiggy has been super-ceded and "Kooky" is on the way out with all the other 1967 Quant clothes). During the rather dull little talk, Greta (I will call her) was limited in vocal range, vocabulary and personal experience. She reached her heights of emphasis when she told us that Twiggy took *an hour to make up her eyes* each morning. When Greta had finished her talk, instead of wasting precious moments of the 12 to 15 minutes allotment talking about Twiggy I turned the conversation completely by saying: "Greta, you're an intelligent lively girl, what would *you* do with the hour Twiggy uses making up her eyes?" A fascinating conversation developed from this which led quickly through from her genuine motivation for using the time on French vocabulary—French conversation—visits to France—to a revelation that she had in fact been to Lourdes as a helper. After she had told us of some of the tasks she had undertaken, and had given us one or two personal experiences, I invited two of her colleagues to come out and be volunteers for next year's visit. Greta gave them instructions on what she wanted them to do and answered their questions in lively, well-ranged, direct dialogue.

One C.S.E. board bases its whole test on an informal conversation on a topic introduced by the candidate. If an examiner is bound by the limited formula of such an exam (see chart "conversation on candidate's suggested topic") the *total test* could be a vapid and worthless exchange on a topic such as "Twiggy" with the examiner subscribing to the idea that glib, banal and superficial talk is all that is needed in such a test. On this particular occasion the headmaster of the school was present and I was able to point out that a superficial spoken essay might have been avoided if there had been guidance and stimulus long before the day of the actual test.

By the time the test was over Greta had also talked to the audience about her book and had read a passage chosen by the examiner to which she had been led in a brief discussion. Yet when the test was over she came, paper in hand, to enquire: "Aren't you going to hear my conversation?" Written out in the form of an elementary play was the dialogue between herself and a shopkeeper which was her way of interpreting the suggestion in the syllabus of a conversation "meeting a situation". I explained to her, and to the listening teachers, that Greta had already conversed with me, the whole group and the selected two from the audience in a lively exchange on a number of ideas, and that she had "met the situation" in training her Lourdes "helpers". To sum up: preparation and spontaneity are not opposing elements. We can only be truly informative and spontaneous if we have made a subject, a book, play or poem our own. Conversation grows from response to a worth-while stimulus, so we must ensure that our candidates have explored things in depth and breadth in the *years* preceding the exam. This will also help to ensure that examiners are not chosen for their ability to produce "instant talk" but because it could be said of them that they, like Socrates, have "the gift of discerning knowledge in others and of having the power to assist them to bring it to light".

This wholesale examination will, if we do not set our sights high, give far too many teachers the illusion that they are succeeding as examiners simply because they are able—in adolescent jargon—to "chat-up" the candidates in superficial small talk and then translate this trivial exercise on to mark sheets to prove that the correct administrative action has been taken and that they have produced ranking and grading acceptable to the statisticians.

Some of the boards are making the examination an enriching experience by demanding at least three different kinds of speech situation with one, at least, based on a subject properly investigated by the boys and girls themselves. One or two of the syllabuses which, on first reading seem widely based and thorough in their coverage of the subject, narrow the experience down considerably when one realises this is a catalogue from which *one* subject only is chosen. For example, it would be possible in one region for a child to opt for the "improvised dialogue with another colleague" on a subject given by the examiner and for this to be the *only test*. Improvisation, useful as it is in drama and speech classes, should, in a *communication test*, be based on something which the child is capable of communicating. In any case imaginative improvisation can arise logically from a project, personal interest, book or poem. In an unrelated improvisation the confident child could take over from a more diffident partner to the possible detriment of the more modest one.

Internal or External Assessors

From the experience of the pilot tests carried out by the E.S.B., at the request of various education authorities, it would certainly be our recommendation that in every internal examination there should be at least a "sample" testing carried out by an external examiner. Otherwise it is logical to assume—and indeed we proved it in our pilot tests—that the teachers who know the least about the subject and have the lowest standards award the highest marks. Conversely, the most knowledgeable and exacting teachers give their own candidates, mark-for-mark, a lower result because of their higher standard. In any case, as the whole subject is wide open for experiment and investigation, any teacher might learn a great deal from external examiners who have visited other schools and other regions, and are capable of making the group examination an enriching experience for all concerned.

Our experience also suggests that teachers are often better assessors with children whom they do not know than with those they have taught. Too often the assessment of their own pupils is based on some preconceived judgement or expectation. They mark on what they expect to hear rather than on what they actually hear. This perhaps points to an interchange of neighbouring teachers in the role of examiners. It raises many problems, not least for the short-staffed head who has to agree to a general post and see members of his permanent staff become part-time peripatetic examiners.

This complicated administrative machinery is only worth setting in motion for a challenging stimulating examination which is richly relevant to the child's experience and growth. Most of the C.S.E. oral tests carried out so far have merely exposed the too-little-too-late quality of the courses leading up to them; and because examiners were anxious to encourage even the weediest of growths, too many little pale shoots had to be accepted, struggling from undernourished soil to get to the light. What is needed in this subject is a two-spit-deep preparation of the nurturing ground.

A spoken English examination in the fifth year of secondary-school

life should not be a little addendum to a more assertive and demanding written English paper but it should be a means whereby our
young adults can demonstrate what fifteen or sixteen years of living
and learning have done for them.

Assessment

Reading the *Examinations Bulletin* No. 3 we could easily be thrown
back to square one by this, rather universally held, idea: "Much of
the evidence available about oral examinations suggests that it is a
method of examining which has low reliability and validity unless
used by a skilled examiner for a quite precise purpose."

This, as was pointed out by Astryx in the *Times Educational Supplement* (1st April, 1966), is devastating when one reflects soberly on
the small number of skilled examiners compared with the large
number of prospective candidates and the uncertainty of purpose of
the C.S.E. or English teaching in general.

On the other hand, I would add that there is a great danger in
having a "quite precise purpose" handed out to, or by, the skilled
examiner. If the purpose is narrowly "precise" (e.g. the aural comprehension tests with written answers) are we not going to lose the
breadth and therefore the educational value of such tests and limit
the preceding teaching.

Again to quote Astryx verbatim:

> English is a bundle of very different techniques. Essay writing, reading
> aloud, speaking to the teacher, holding one's own in group discussion, and
> talking privately to friends are skills of a rather different kind, employing
> different registers of the language, and variously affected by such matters as
> social class.
>
> But more than technique is involved. Probably most English teachers see
> their main job as a development of the child's reasoning power and
> imagination. But even this is an ambiguous goal. Should one measure it by
> the seriousness and importance of the subjects the child can handle
> competently or by the degree of naturalness and spontaneous interest the
> child will show in what are, perhaps, trivial and unrewarding subjects. Who,
> in any case, is to judge seriousness and importance?

The short answer from E.S.B. examiners would be that we must
accept the responsibility and the challenge. All that Astryx says is
highly relevant to the judgements we must make, but the last para-
graph is also relevant to music and art where somehow we manage

to find reasonably satisfactory agreement between examiners and adjudicators dealing with established examinations and festivals. After the E.S.B. pilot scheme C.S.E. tests held in different parts of the country with panels of moderators drawn mostly from English staffs of schools and colleges, a summing up of methods and assessment was compiled by Elizabeth Henry (Principal Lecturer in the Speech Department, College of Education, Aberdeen). In it she reached the following conclusions:

> The close agreement in marking between examiners and moderators makes it reasonable to affirm that we are marking the same thing.
> The fact that agreement was not so great when no speech specialists were on the panel of moderators points to the necessity of training and experience in potential examiners.
> Since the correlation was equally high in widely separated parts of the country, the possibility of bias on the part of these examiners in favour of one pronunciation rather than another is eliminated. (Geographical range from Aberdeen to Plymouth.)
> The overall distribution of grades was as follows:
> A: (distinction) B: (credit) C: (V.G. pass) D: (G. pass) E: (pass)
>   4·3%   14·8%   21·3%   17%   22·1%
> Fail or ungraded: 20·5%

(This, of course, would be a depressingly high failure rate in a practical C.S.E. test but we must remember that this test was carried out on candidates who had had on the whole, either a crash-course or no course leading up to the test a year before the C.S.E. was, in fact, in operation. C. B.)

> Agreement between examiners' marks and the average of the moderators' marks was as follows:
>
> | | |
> |---|---|
> | Total agreement | 51% |
> | Difference of 1 grade | 42·25% |
> | Difference of 2 grades | 5·5% |
> | Difference of 3 grades | 1·25% |

In more than 93% of all cases the grade allocated by the examiners and moderators either agreed exactly or disagreed by only one grade.

> The correlation coefficients of the examiners' ranking as compared with the moderators' average is as follows:
> +0·96   +0·94   +0·94   +0·94   +0·93   +0·93
> +0·92   +0·90   +0·90   +0·89   +0·87   +0·86
> +0·81   +0·78   +0·56

The group of moderators which had the lowest correlation with the examiners' ranking was the only group which contained no specialists who had experience in examining speech and drama.

> Three of the lower correlation groups belonged to the Aberdeen examination where numbers in groups were small. It is worth noticing that the moderators' marks tended to draw much closer to one another and to the examiners' assessment after the first three or four candidates although there was no sort of consultation at any time.

But here, quoted from Miss Henry's report, are four candidates' marks given by a group of moderators who had had no previous experience of teaching or examining *spoken* English.

	Candidate	Range of moderators' marks	Moderators' average	Examination mark	Final grade
	A	8–20	14	17·5	V.G. pass (C)
Max. mark	B	11–20	15	14·5	G. pass (D)
25	C	11–20	14	14·1	G. pass (D)
	D	11·5–22	18	18·1	Credit (B)

In each of these cases the candidate had been failed by at least one moderator and given Distinction by another! One candidate (A) belonged to the group where the correlation between moderators' and examiners' marking was lowest.

Miss Henry concludes:

> It is not claimed that this four-fold test is perfect in content or in methods of assessment. It *is* claimed that spoken English can be measured by fully-trained and experienced teachers, and that, properly administered, this test is relevant to life, deriving its value from:
> (a) The variety of speaking situations devised for the candidate in the course of the test.
> (b) The reciprocity of a participating group.
> (c) The open-ended nature of the test which gives the candidate an opportunity to show his responsive listening throughout the session.
> (d) The chance to present facts with which he is thoroughly familiar, illustrated with visual aids.

Judgement Through Experience

Over the fifteen years the E.S.B. in connection with its own series of examinations (co-ordinating exams, demonstration exams, examiner training sessions or actual exam work with trainee-examiners present) has created opportunities for examiners to compare their results. Here judgements are more demanding since the margin of error in dealing with a multiple-stage examination is necessarily wide. Yet even so amongst the experienced examiners agreement is practically total and after a few examining sessions, newcomers to this job (provided they have the necessary training, background and basic educational philosophy) soon themselves subscribe to this high correlation reached by the experienced examiners.

Clearly then the most pressing needs for the immediate future are:

(a) In-service training courses for teachers at all levels.

(b) Week-end courses for examiners.

(c) Demonstration examinations for potential examiners.

(d) Co-ordinating examinations prior to the dispersal of separate examiners to their allotted tasks.

(e) "Post-mortem" meetings of examiners to compare their experiences and their results.

(f) Meetings of external examiners working in different parts of the country to exchange views and co-ordinate their marks.

Tape-recording Testing

Some of the C.S.E. panels are assessing their candidates for spoken English on tape-recordings (Brighton experiment 1963) but whatever claims may be made that this increases objectivity and reliability, we could not support it in any way. In the E.S.B. tests the physical presence of the speakers, their facial expression, handling of visual aids and gear, and the interchange of thoughts with the listeners are acknowledged to be part of communication and inseparable from the sequence of sounds. In a true speech relationship, pauses which appear to be mental gaps or inertia on the "tape", could in actual fact be full of meaning.

In their report the Southern Region for C.S.E. summed up their opinions (which are supported by Arthur Wise, formerly chief examiner for the London G.C.E.), as follows:

1. The disembodied voice cannot possibly be assessed in the absence of gestures; attitude; projection of the personality into the "conversation"; evidence of audience contact.

2. Some voices reproduce better than others on magnetic tape.

3. The presence of the microphone and recorder inhibits communication.

4. First-class equipment and technical skill cannot be assured.

CHAPTER 8

Vocational Examinations in Spoken English for Students in Technical Colleges, Commerce and Industry

EVERY adult student entering the business or industrial world is called on to inform, explain, instruct or demonstrate at some level and to receive and act on other people's information, explanations, instructions and demonstrations. Yet this important aspect of living and learning is almost wholly neglected not only in our schools but in our colleges.

Millions of pounds are spent on technical equipment for colleges and factories but we cannot measure how much money is wasted in the wide gap between expert technical knowledge and the skill of knowing how to put that information across. Students leave school with low standards of oral communication and there is practically no check on their powers of aural comprehension. Very little research has been done on the amount of information which is heard but not truly received. However, we must not presume to criticise aural comprehension unless we take full responsibility for better quality in oral communication.

All this is of vital importance, not only to the prosperity and productivity of our country but for harmony in personal and industrial relationships.

The English Speaking Board is seeking, through its series of examinations designed for those who have left school, to direct the attention of the colleges and industrial training schools to the necessity for giving real training in the skills of oral communication with all that is implied in the reciprocal business of aural comprehension.

In order to give the subject prestige and to make it earn and keep

76

a place in the jealously guarded time-table, it is important to have an end-product—an examination.

Unlike other examinations in the tertiary stages of education these tests are not designed to record facts the candidate has memorised and absorbed, but rather to find out what the student has discovered, practised, contended with, made his own and enjoyed.

The exams are ranged to accommodate recently left-school students attending a technical or commercial college, day-release students in part-time classes, more mature students completing a two- or three-year concentrated course, adults in control of groups and business executives with managerial responsibilities. Those who have already taken the tests—many thousands representing every area in England and parts of Scotland and Wales—include a wide range of professions and careers: pre-nursing students, nursery nurses, hairdressers, shorthand-typists, receptionists, secretaries, demonstrators, caterers; police cadets, builders, engineers (electrical, motor, mining), draughtsmen, civil service officials, students of business studies, etc.

These students of all ages come from backgrounds which vary socially, culturally and linguistically. Yet all have a common need— the desire to be able to communicate more effectively.

The exams are substantially the same pattern as all the other E.S.B. grades except that in this case there is no memorised interpretation of literature. As in the other exams the personal project—very often a highly skilled demonstration of a particular process with its relevant gear—is the most important part of the test. Spoken English is not a frill tacked on to the course, we do in fact quite often hold the exam in the appropriate "workshop" with the cookers, benches, typewriters and machines near at hand for the relevant demonstrations. After the prescribed talks candidates are grouped in twos and threes in verbal combat, or they answer pertinent questions from their colleagues, tutors and the examiners.

In these examinations the reading is prepared and practised before-hand from a literature book of the candidate's own choice and this is followed by a selection made by the examiner. Informal talk arises from the book's interest, and here again the listening group makes its contribution of enquiry and comment. It is one of the elements of the E.S.B. test that fellow candidates are not considered rivals; interests, experiences, even the "stage-management" of the props for the personal projects are shared. All this underlines the basic idea that good personal relationships depend on good personal communication. There is no question of elbowing one another out in a competitive race. The morbid picture of the arm crooked round a book to exclude the possible "copier" is a symbol of the worst kind of Dickensian education; it has no part in our open-plan concept of education.

In Table 1, taken at random from a hundred technical college E.S.B. reports, is a list of the personal projects presented by students from the General Studies Department and the Demonstrators and Catering department of one college. As will be seen, the candidates show a liberal choice of subject for they can, if they wish, choose a personal interest which may be an engrossing occupation of their leisure time.

The right-hand column shows the student's occupation at the conclusion of the course.

TABLE 1

Course	Personal project	Visual aids	Subsequent vocation
General Studies	Historic reporting on Caligula, Caractacus and Boadicea (as if happening now)	Maps of battle-ground and boundaries	Junior reporter on local newspaper. Ambition to become foreign correspondent
General Studies	Shakespeare at work in the theatre	Model of Globe Theatre made by the candidate	Actor with Bristol Old Vic. At present on tour in America
General Studies	British reptiles kept by the speaker	Live specimens shown	Career in zoology
General Studies	Some aspects of Greek Architecture	Spontaneous blackboard drawings	Architecture student at a College of Advanced Technology

TABLE I (*cont.*)

Course	Personal project	Visual aids	Subsequent vocation
Receptionists. Eight candidates joined together for a combined project	Imaginary Hotel: "Agincourt". Each took one part of the whole	Each of the eight had relevant visual aids: carpeting, curtains, wall-paper, kitchen equipment etc. which were integrated	All are now employed in first-class hotels in Great Britain and the Continent
Disabled adult student attending evening classes. Has taken 3 E.S.B. Vocational exams and Public Speaking	1. Glove-making 2. Home-making 3. Gas Board, etc.	1. Leathers, tools and gloves used in demonstra-tions 2. Diagrams and pictures 3. Charts, etc.	Has become Chairman of the local Gas Board and is an accom-plished public speaker for women's causes, etc.
Demonstrator (2 exams)	1. Campanology 2. Honey	1. Charts of "pulling" sequences 2. Samples of various kinds of honey, mead, etc.	Received a direct commission into the W.R.N.S.
Demonstrator	Regional cookery of the south-west	3 recipes demonstrated (2 partially prepared beforehand)	Demonstrator for the Gas Board
Demonstrator	Potatoes	Charts, samples and pamphlets from the Ministry of Agriculture	Assistant to County Housecraft Adviser
Secretarial Course	Training for fashion modelling	Colleagues as models. Clothes made in the dress-designing department	Now a qualified and successful model

TABLE I (*cont.*)

Course	Personal project	Visual aids	Subsequent vocation
Secretarial Course	Central Park, New York Folk Music	Photographs. Guitar accompaniment ½ minute of a recording	Qualified secretary interested in taking a job in the States
Secretarial Course	Archery	Bows and arrows used in demonstration. Instruction given to members of audience	Qualified secretary with high standards of grooming, deportment and efficiency

Men students from various other departments of technical colleges have demonstrated and explained projects such as rock climbing, judo, the two-stroke and four-stroke engine, safety in mines, modern building materials, programming computers, aspects of local government, glacial erosion and deposition, the work of Louis Pasteur, discovery of insulin, circulation of carbon and nitrogen, the nature and transmission of sound, electromagnets and their uses, the turbine engine, solving the traffic problem, the concept of a vector, the use of the theodolite, the fall of the Third Republic in France, the growth of the Trade Union movement, dangers of drugs, etc.

These are a random selection of subjects selected from several hundred projects.

It is difficult to measure the influence this kind of learning and testing has on the individual. Briefly, it should ensure that the student

(a) enlarges his horizons and those of others,
(b) moves outward in the course of his investigation,
(c) goes deeper into the thinking process,
(d) builds understanding into himself through practical application and communication,
(e) develops in individual personality,
(f) increases in social confidence,

(g) becomes more appreciative of others,

(h) listens generously and actively,

(i) cultivates the ability to select from a mass of material the essential points in presentation,

(j) finds through experience how to approach people and books to get information,

(k) marshals his material and presents it in an orderly way,

(l) discovers that clarity in oral communication demands basic techniques.

In the limited space of two or three paragraphs it is difficult to show the endless repercussions and ramifications resulting from this thematic approach to learning. But there must be firm and challenging *end-products*. A paste and paper "folio" collected over a period of time will not in itself build understanding into a student. He must know how to select, marshal and present his material. The best single test of whether a subject is grasped is if it can be communicated to others. If it is communicated *orally* the student has the responsibility of presentation and projection—immediate tests of courtesy and clarity. Aural comprehension is implicit in every operation since any breakdown in communication is challenged at once by those who have the responsibility of receiving and understanding through aural response.

From the thousands of "case-histories" recorded and unrecorded in the fifteen years of E.S.B. work I am citing one in detail to show not only the excitement of the enquiry and discovery but the many skills which were *fully used* and developed through the single project. There is no vague "self-expression" here, nor has the student merely been a happy onlooker or an academic recorder. She has contended, adventured, coped, adapted herself to other people and recognised and tried to understand their skills.

PERSONAL PROJECT: *The New Mersey Tunnel*, given by a 17-year-old technical college student. (Introductory Vocational exam.)

Time allowed for the talk: 5 minutes.

Visual aids. Charts showing the sinking of the vertical shafts—the bed of the river—general plan, etc. (drawn accurately by the girl herself—mathematical precision and manual dexterity were needed here).

The talk given on the day of the spoken English examination described the siting, planning, designing and building of the new tunnel and the many problems involved. Her manner was authoritative but humble, she gave clear evidence that each point mentioned could in itself be the subject of a whole lecture. One surprising item of information was that one of the mechanical diggers had been brought from Pakistan.

After the talk I asked her how she had got her information and immediately she opened out on to the most interesting account of all, *her* interdisciplinary enquiry. (She, of course, would not want to give it such a high-sounding title!) As I was in the middle of writing this chapter and was already wondering how I could find "ciphers to this great accompt" to show the endeavour and interaction of subjects and people of at least 5000 students, I asked her if she would jot down for me after the examination the many people to whom she had talked and the paths which she had followed in her preparation of this project, I will use this one girl as the "cipher" to represent a host of others: "into a thousand parts divide one man". I would also ask the reader to fill in between the lines of this understated personal letter to me. It arrived neatly written, perfectly spelt and punctuated three days after the day of the examination.

People to whom I talked in preparing my project on
The New Mersey Tunnel

I decided to do my personal project for the English Speaking Board examination on the subject "The New Mersey Tunnel". Mr. Lavery, my speech tutor at the Technical College, arranged an interview for me at the Town Hall Borough Engineer's Department.

On arrival at the Town Hall I was introduced to a member of the Borough Engineer's Department who took me to his office. I explained what information I required and why I wanted it. He wanted to know about the examination and how it was related to the course which I am studying. After introducing my side of the subject I sat down and I was given all the information I required for my project. This included information on the plans, construction, cost, work, traffic relief and use of the New Mersey Tunnel in great detail. I was shown all of the documents concerning the tunnel since 1958, and also the detailed scaled plans of the actual tunnel and ventilation shafts. A street map on a wall in the office showed the site of the new tunnel and the approach roads which are to be built up through the Wirral. Everyone was very helpful and gave me great encouragement as well as the facts which I wanted. With the assurance that I could contact the office at any time, I left my one and a half hour interview with pages of shorthand notes to transcribe.

When I had transcribed the notes from my previous interview I set out to talk to the men actually working on the site. My first visit was profitless as I was not suitably dressed. On my second visit I wore slacks, sweater and knee-high boots to meet the thick mud on the site. I interviewed the foreman first and he gave me permission to talk to the men and ask questions.

I spoke to miners, engineers, crane drivers, electricians and many others. I found out about the pumping system to keep the tunnel clear, the types of jobs, the actual construction of the tunnel, the work of the various pieces of mechanical equipment, and what was probably most interesting of all, the conditions in which the men work and the many nationalities of the people involved with the tunnel, both on the administrative staff and the actual labourers.

The thing which struck me most was the different ways in which I was received. Both at the Town Hall and the worksite I was treated courteously and all of my questions were answered thoroughly and with interest. I found, however, that I asked all of my questions from a different point of view at the worksite than I did at the Borough Engineer's Department. There is a great deal of difference between the planning genius at the Town Hall and the specialised labourers who actually do the constructing of the tunnel. All questions have to be framed on this basis.

At the worksite and the Town Hall I found that, as well as obtaining all the information relevant to my project, I learned a great deal about the many levels of specialised and technical knowledge which are needed for a major job such as the construction of the second Mersey crossing.

I shall not hesitate to contact the Town Hall again if I need any information. I also have an open invitation to the worksite to see how the job is progressing. I do not think it really necessary to add that I shall be accepting this invitation many times in the near future. This project which started as a theme for a five minute talk for an examination has become a major interest and it will be so for many years to come.

Brief Analysis of the Educative Values

Triggering-off point: E.S.B. exam—speech and drama and English lecturer.

Personal contact and discussion with: lecturers, borough engineer, officials in the borough engineer's office, foreman, crane drivers, miners, builders and excavators.

Skills used: written letters and records, telephone conversations, interviews, shorthand records of conversation, transcription of shorthand, typing, scale drawings, reading of plans and maps.

Subjects linked through the project: English (spoken and written), secretarial studies, geography, history (of Merseyside), geology, mathematics, various sciences and aspects of engineering, local government, trade unions, social studies, economics, traffic problems, national planning and expenditure, air pollution, draughtsmanship, administration (at many levels), road constructions (leading to the tunnel), drainage, machinery and tools used, radar transmission, maintenance, etc.

Personal development: improvement in all the skills listed above— social competence in making appointments and conducting inter- views—tact in approaching different people in different ways and speaking in different registers—sense of humour—consideration when using other people's time—courtesy in acknowledging this in speech and writing—sensibility in respecting "the worker" whether he is a creative genius, a top-level executive or an honest labourer— increased confidence in communicating information to colleagues— courtesy and clarity in asking questions—growth from student to "citizen" through accepting responsibility and appreciating the responsibilities of others.

Maurice Wiggin, reviewing a television programme on American and British methods discussed by The Professor of Comparative Education at Columbia and The Professor of Comparative Education at London University, sums up a sound educational philosophy (*Sunday Times*, 23rd April, 1967).

> If cramming really produced superior citizens, or, what is far more to the point, happier people—if there were any discernible correlation between academic prowess and human completeness—there might be some point in it. But what we saw here was the fatally divisive effect produced by the unacknowledged and insidious penetration of class consciousness into education. Euphemisms aside, education is used to get children out of the fish-and-chip society into the steak-and-chip society; any side-effects such as a taste for culture are incidental. If the only object of cramming is to produce eager-beaver rat-racers who read book reviews instead of books, shape their lives on the values of the glossy magazine ads, and live in a dreadful atmosphere of mingled pride and fear, we are wasting as asset far more precious than money.
>
> And this is where television could step in to redress the balance. . . .
>
> . . . A good deal was said about the need for discipline—the famed rigour of British education. Granted that any accomplishment demands a discipline —innumerable uneducated people eagerly submit to one, *when they find something that interests them:* become accomplished and even scholarly gardeners, fishermen, photographers, film fans, sailors, music lovers, bird watchers, botanists, hot-rod tuners, philatelists, archeologists. But academic disciplines are for the few, just as a taste for abstract thought is for the few. Cramming children who are unripe for it is as cruel as battery farming, which it closely resembles.

CHAPTER 9

Conclusion

EDUCATION profits and suffers from abnormal swings of the pendulum. In the last few years the pendulum has swung—commendably one would like to say—towards "mime and movement", "creative drama", "dance drama", "creative writing" and "creative art". Nothing could be more worth-while when the teachers who are guiding the lessons are fulfilled human beings with high standards, rich experience and special communicative skills. But those of us who visit schools, and indeed colleges of education, are forced to admit that much that we see in "creative drama", "creative movement" and "creative art" is merely formless self-indulgence where too few demands are made on imaginative observation and the muscular control and practice necessary for its interpretation.

There is a danger of this kind of effervescence in the sudden change of attitude towards the teaching of English. Belatedly, but far too vaguely, there is a necessary swing away from the predominance of *written* English to a general approval of anything and everything which comes under the umbrella term: "oracy". "Language flow", "oral creativity", "spoken English", "linguistics for schools", "aural comprehension", "thematic approach" . . . books on the subject are pouring out, some are excellent but some are written by people who have never practised what they now so fervently preach. Several of the books written for secondary school courses aim very little higher than the disjointed small talk which the children hear at "Juke Box Jury" level and there is a danger, if we do not set our sights high *now*, of establishing this kind of standard for the C.S.E. spoken English test.

We must bear in mind in our efforts to raise the standard of English in this country that any worth-while course in spoken English should not only develop the pupil's oral communication but should create more complete and enquiring human beings who will *want* to read

85

and write more imaginatively and more precisely. A good step forward would be to remove the present barrier between English language and English literature. Even in the primary stages children should be surrounded by, and personally possess, *books* not "readers" and they should be taught English by people who can not only use the language functionally but can *interpret* it imaginatively through voice, speech (and where appropriate), movement. Literature can only be fully enjoyed if it can be "read with the ears" and this is only possible if at every stage it is given vocal life. Silent reading can then become a total imaginative experience.

So far our training of English teachers has been an entirely academic business and it is to the credit of a host of English teachers that, in spite of the sedentary and sometimes boring atmosphere of the lecture halls in universities and colleges of education, they have managed, through their own native talent and enthusiasm, to acquire certain communicative skills. But this should be the responsibility of the English departments and should not be left to the Institutes of Education to have to give crash courses to intending teachers too little and too late.

The valuable teachers of English, a splendid and inspiring minority, are able to use the voice, speech and physical body to interpret their perceptive response to experience. They are able to transform printed symbols into vital and aesthetically satisfying spoken forms. Their reward is the engrossed listening of their pupils and in turn a reciprocal vocal response and exchange of ideas from the pupils themselves.

The highly critical reports on the teaching and examining of English issued by the Schools Council and echoed in the educational journals and national press have given an impetus which has led to a reforming spirit. Some of the reforms show in more liberal and wider-based English "O" level papers. But as Esmor Jones, secretary of N.A.T.E., points out so rightly in *Where?*, a "pass" in English language should be an added bonus for the child who has read with critical enjoyment and shared his thoughts and discoveries at home and school in oral exchange.

The only possible way to improve the quality of English all round is for children to hear and speak good English. It is of secondary importance that they can put the descriptive grammatical tags on to the parts of speech, or now the more fashionable linguistic labels. Those of us who speak reasonably grammatically do not do so because we learnt how to analyse and parse (though we may not be any the worse off for the exercise) but because we *heard* and *read* English which was not malformed nor debased. Some of us were fortunate in coming from homes where tales were told, songs were sung, poems were spoken, ideas exchanged and jokes shared. We profited too (if we had imaginative English teachers) from being at school before the pendulum swung violently away from "learning by heart". Because we spoke *aloud* we learnt how to bring out the subtleties of meaning through intonation, rhythm, inflection, tone and tone-colour.

John Grigg, commenting in the *Guardian* on 11th May, 1967 on the previously mentioned article by Esmor Jones, says:

> The teaching of English in Britain's schools—both state and independent— has long been a disgrace. Language is the indispensable basis for coherent thought and those who learn their own language inadequately go through life with a crippling disability. At all levels the British speak their language less well than many other nations, including most conspicuously the French. Frenchmen on the whole speak their language not merely with ease but with style, observing its nuances and choosing their words with affectionate care. English is a greater language than French, but no one would judge so from comparing the talk of average Englishmen and average Frenchmen.

Although few of us would feel confident to make assertions on the "average Englishman" and the "average Frenchman" there is much more than a germ of truth in John Grigg's stricture.

We can improve this state of affairs, not by having more rigorous or more liberal "Eng. Lang." papers, but by giving attention to, practice in and assessment of *spoken* English at every stage from nursery school to university. This means equipping every teacher, whatever his subject, with voice and speech which commands respect and response. Over and above this, every teacher of English, if he intends to put literature at the centre of his teaching, should have a practical training in the language arts. Nuance of meaning in literature can only be communicated through imaginatively motivated muscles. Speech and movement must not be separated arts but equal partners in aesthetic and functional communication.

APPENDIXES

1. SPOKEN ENGLISH EXAMINATIONS IN THE COLLEGES OF EDUCATION

THERE is a spate of books, pamphlets and articles on the teaching of English. High-sounding phrases abound: "working from children's interests", "free and creative writing", "thematic-contextual approach", "growth of the imagination", "functional, as opposed to, textbook grammar", "literature relevant to life", "creative drama", "creative movement", "interdisciplinary enquiry" and, of course, "oracy".

But how much *time* is allotted in the colleges of education for the basic skills and practice which are necessary for the oral interpretation of the literature which we all agree must be at the centre of the English course? And at a more utilitarian level, how much real training and practice is a teacher given in the highly responsible job of communication of information?

The teaching of English will never be any better than the quality of the teachers themselves. Recently I listened to a student in a college of education giving a dissertation—a very dry and dull one—on the use of closed-circuit television in education. Much expensive "hardware" had been bought for the college and no doubt a little had been learnt about its manipulation. The speaker, who evidently intended to use this apparatus as a means of "bringing English to life", had a narrow range of vocal register, limited resonance, apathetic tone-colour, imprecise and flabby articulation, staccato rhythm, an inexpressive face and a perfunctory stance. During the conversation which followed I learnt that he had two small children of his own, so I asked him (thinking that this would perhaps release his voice and motivate his communication) to say any rhyme, poem or story

88

which he would tell to his pre-school children. This request was met with a blank stare and then a mumbled, "I don't know any". If this were an isolated case it would be unfair to cite it as an example. But after acting as external examiner in spoken English in twenty-two colleges of education over a period of ten years I feel depressed and concerned at the generally low standard of "oracy" of our teachers-in-training. Moreover, it should be borne in mind that the people heard by external examiners are those who choose to do speech and drama as a main or advanced subject. The students not heard by the external examiner for spoken English who have chosen other disciplines as a main subject may be better oral communicators, but one can deduce that there must also be many students in the colleges, never tested at all, who fall below the somewhat elementary standard of the present spoken English test.

This is not a criticism of the lecturers but of the system. Too many of the students entering a college of education have had to keep their noses—if not on a grindstone—at least not far from their academic reading and writing for the necessary university—geared "O" and "A" level work. Too many of them have returned from their grammar schools each day to a high tea-homework-television pattern of life which has given little experience in social interaction or aesthetic use of language. The school time-table has included little or no movement, creative drama, reading aloud, verse speaking, discussion or debate, though many schools achieve high standards with the enthusiasts in the extra-curricula societies. Consequently, with the silent reading and writing programme a persistent pattern is established throughout the secondary school: the visual recognition vocabulary is larger than the producible written one and the producible written one is vastly bigger than the producible *oral* vocabulary. The cure for this is not to prescribe a dose of "speech-training". It is a much more fundamental demand. Children from the earliest age right through primary and secondary school should have imaginative experience of movement and speech. Speech, in fact, is thought translated into *movement* and the two disciplines, creative movement and creative speech, are indivisible.

But the lecturers in the colleges of education rarely have students with such a training. It is far too late at this stage to make major change in the muscular, vocal and speech habits of their students.

They do what they can, many of them with remarkable success. Of course, in nearly every college there are the gifted few and the ardent plodders who make the most of their equipment, but a vast number of students have neither the imagination nor the incentive to realise that the business of oral communication should be their basic professional skill. The only way to make this fully realised is to establish systematic training and testing in spoken communication for every student at each stage in the three-year course. Time must be found for it.

Here are reports from two colleges of education where time has been made. Every student in the college, irrespective of the particular discipline she is studying, is tested by an external examiner in spoken English. The effect on the development of personality and on the quality of teaching has been marked, but the two writers of the articles would want to say, I feel sure, that much greater heights would be reached if the grammar schools accepted some responsibility for this training from the first year to the sixth.

1a. ACCOUNT OF THE SPOKEN ENGLISH EXAMINATIONS HELD AT SEDGLEY PARK COLLEGE OF EDUCATION, PRESTWICH, MANCHESTER

By Eunice Woodfield

"Evil communications corrupt good manners." And poor oral communication prevents efficient teaching. This is why it is essential that ALL teachers in training should be made to realise the truth and importance of this. Yet, in my experience, few do unless they have had training in spoken English *before they come to college.*

It was for this reason that in 1964 we decided to have ALL the first-year students examined in spoken English, by external examiners and not just to examine those who chose to do speech and drama for a main-course subject.

Why have an examination? And why have it externally examined? Weren't the usual oral communication lectures that we had in college adequate to make the students aware of the value of good oral communication in the classroom? No, they were not.

Reports were frequently coming in from other college tutors, and headteachers and staffs of schools that students were severely handi-capped in Teaching Practice because of the inability to communicate effectively through the spoken word. I used all my powers of per-suasion to make students realise the seriousness of this state of affairs, but with little result. Because of ignorance of the content and disciplines of the subject they would not give any thought, let alone practice, to the *technique* of oral communication.

There were various reasons for this. Some students were apathetic. They had never heard their own speech critically, nor had they received any instruction or help in their schools. Consequently they were incapable of judging how effective their own speech was as a teaching instrument.

Some were prejudiced about modifying a very strong—and perhaps defiant—local accent. "Ah've lived in Bolton all me life an' ah'm going to teach there. The kids will understand me, and ah'll under-stand the kids. What more can anyone want?"

Others were frightened because they realised their ability to com-municate orally was weak and as they had no confidence in their being any hope of improvement they did no practice. They were also, through insecurity, determined to avoid any possible exposure of their oral weakness in public. A few, very few, students were lazy; some of the energetic ones were ill-organised, they entered enthusiasti-cally into every College social activity and had little energy or inclination left for the necessary daily speech practice.

Although the reasons for doing little or no voice and speech work were many and varied, there was one external factor which influenced a great many students—speech was not an *examinable* subject. No matter how many instances I gave them of students who had failed to get a distinction in Practice of Education, because oral com-munication fell short of distinction standard, each individual thought that this could not possibly apply to her. I realised that the majority of my students needed some stronger incentive to practise than I had already given them.

For a good many years I had been interested in the work done by E.S.B. and had entered school-children and technical college part-time students for the Board's examinations. I knew that if we had in our College an internal examination based on the E.S.B. pattern nearly every one of the students who did little or no speech practice would do some, and the standard of oral communication could not help but improve. Moreover, it would underline the point that this business of "oracy" belonged to all subjects.

I also realised that if the students were *internally* examined, the status of the examination and the value of the certificate would not be as high as it would if an award were based on the national standards of external examiners.

When I suggested to the Principal (Sister Mary Regis) the idea that we might have an internal examination modelled on E.S.B. lines and examined by E.S.B. external examiners she readily agreed to arrange this for the end of the academic year (1964).

We decided that all the first-year students should be examined. This caused great consternation. A small group of students came to see me saying that they thought their speech was quite good enough for the classroom, and that for them to take an examination in spoken English was wasting their time and the examiner's. They also disagreed with the form of the examination. I knew that their complaints and arguments were only a façade to hide their fears. I explained to the students that the examination was an experiment but this did not make the students less resentful. The general feeling was "Why should we be picked out to be guinea pigs?" Nevertheless, the majority of the students worked. Out of 110 candidates ten were awarded distinction, twenty failed.

The Principal decided that the examination was an educational success, and that all first-year students in future should take a similar examination at the end of June.

The following year the new students, initiated from the start, accepted the examination as part of the general College pattern and there was no resentment. Seventeen students gained distinction and out of 138 candidates only three failed. The twenty students who had failed in the previous year were re-examined. They had been given detailed written notes of their weaknesses and potential strength. They all passed.

The Speech work in College is time-tabled as Oracy, and each group has fifty minutes once in each six-day week. As the groups are made up of from twenty to forty-five students, this is quite inadequate, and our scheme of work has to be carefully planned and heavily "subsidised" out of my free time and theirs.

In the first term attention is paid to the student's own vocal technique, because this is the term of the first teaching practice. After teaching practice, the students are given details of their end-of-year examination, and demonstrations of spoken English work ranging from 8-year-old primary school children to that of our own College students are given (personal projects, reading aloud, acted poems, creative drama, verse-speaking poems and ballads, choral speaking, scripted drama, etc.).

In the second term we divide the classes into smaller groups and have *informal* discussions with individual readings of poetry, prose and drama shared by the other members of the group; this is followed by constructive criticism. Later time is allotted for learning how to take the Chair at a public lecture, the conduct of committees and how to give votes of thanks.

In the third term we have discussions on C.S.E. spoken English examinations, and we show how ALL teachers share the responsibility from the Reception class onwards. I stress the fact that C.S.E. examinations are teacher-controlled and *teacher-examined*. Talks are given on some of the forms that C.S.E. spoken English take. A "mock" examination is held, local schools sending us children. The children's ages range from 8 to 15 years; the younger ones demonstrate E.S.B. grade examinations ranging from Introductory up to Junior 3. The senior school children do C.S.E. work. Our students mark at these "mock" examinations, and when the children have gone, the marks awarded are discussed. Listening generously but critically to children makes them humble and more zealous about their own shortcomings!

In addition, students work at their own personal examination work, coming individually by appointment for any help or advice they need.

Tutors of other subjects in College often give students valuable help in the preparation of projects, in tape-recording and the showing of slides; and special Speech demonstrations have been arranged for the Education Department.

We are greatly indebted to the local schools who allow me to experiment and demonstrate with groups of their children.

The spoken English examinations at College last for four days, from 9 a.m. to 5.30 p.m. each day, with two examiners each working in separate rooms. The time allowed is approximately 18 minutes per student. Time-consuming? Yes! But it may prove to be the most valuable 18 minutes in the student's academic life.

As this is an internal examination, the College authorities pay the examiner's fees and provide special certificates. Each first-year student is required to pay something towards these expenses.

Although many students are very apprehensive at the idea of having a participating audience, they find, at the actual examination, that the listening group is helpful and stimulating. Members of staff who are free often come in to the examination to listen, and we frequently have tutors from other colleges. Thus the oral communication has become the link for all the different disciplines and the speech and drama lecturer finds she is not working in isolation as so often happens.

Since we had our first examination two other colleges have followed our example, and another one is carefully considering doing so. But we feel that our greatest achievement is one which is difficult to measure: it is the change of *attitude* of the students towards spoken English for it also means a change of attitude towards *people*. It is not long before this changed attitude makes its mark in the classroom.

A teacher who can hold the interest of children and stimulate them to further endeavour generates happiness.

1b. SPOKEN ENGLISH IN NOTRE DAME COLLEGE OF EDUCATION, MOUNT PLEASANT, LIVERPOOL
By Sister Thérèse Boddington

For a long time I have felt the great need of some form of speech work for all who are to be teachers. If the Newsom Report with its emphasis on spoken English and its place in "the personal development and social competence of the pupil" is to be implemented, then the first requirement is to supply teachers who are aware of the importance of speech, and by "speech" I refer to the ability to speak fluently, "easily, clearly and with interest", as the report puts it. Unless a teacher's powers of communication are developed, she will be useless in the profession, no matter how great her academic qualifications.

This concern made me anxious to have in the curriculum for all first-year students at least some provision by which speech could be taught and examined.

The number of students following a main course in Drama is negligible compared with the number of students in the College. Inevitably in the course of their work these drama students are helped in oral work; it is the other students who need help, for in their education prior to College hardly any of them have done any speech work, and hardly any have ever even done much "talking" in school, because so much emphasis is laid on written work.

This is one of the problems involved in the early College training of the prospective teacher. She has had little practice in oral communication, in discussion, logical thinking, exposition and—not least —in reading aloud, or at least reading aloud with interest. The quality of being a good "narrator" is most useful for a teacher, especially in these days of competition from excellent audio-visual aids. With a full development of her speech faculties a teacher can be a vital audio-visual aid herself, and because of her personality a much more influential one.

I felt that our College should show its concern about the speech of teachers by taking a positive stand on the matter, and when I approached the Principal I had no difficulty in getting her to agree that all first-year students from then on should be obliged to do some form of speech work followed by an examination.

In my first year on the College staff I introduced the English Speaking Board Examination first for those who chose to do it: twenty students availed themselves of the opportunity. In the next two years about 240 first-year students did the English Speaking Board Examination, and about twenty second- and third-year students elected to do a second grade.

I chose the English Speaking Board Examination because its format seems specially suited to teachers in training. An essential part of the examination is the presence of a group of fellow students, who are to be examined during the same session, or who may be present purely out of interest. This group provides a natural setting for talking as they are sympathetic to the examinee and act as an audience. This

8

helps considerably in at least two sections of the examination: the reading aloud which demands listeners, who can share the reader's experience, and the talk which may be followed by questions from the audience. This situation is fairly close to that in the classroom and much more relaxed than that in a very formal examination set-up, where the examinee may be "incarcerated" with one examiner, and the communication becomes somewhat precious and rarified.

We set aside one week during the College examinations and had each day a team of three to five English Speaking Board examiners for about four days. Each was allotted a room and examined on an average twenty-four candidates a day. The time-table was planned so that each student's examination time was arranged when she was free from any other College examination.

This large-scale examination took place in 1965 and 1966. In 1967, owing to our Institute of Education's temporarily allowing us to include spoken English as a compulsory part of the English examination, we decided to have the English Speaking Board Examination replaced by an internal assessment. We had requested an external assessment, feeling that this would stress the importance which we feel should be given to the subject, but we did not receive enough support from other colleges.

Since this arrangement, the Institute has now dropped the compulsory English (written or oral) so next year we shall revert to our original plan and return to the English Speaking Board Examination for our first-year students. Even this year we are having about twenty-eight examined by the English Speaking Board, as these students want an external examination as well as the internal assessment.

It has been my experience, during this interim year, that the standard of work, particularly in the speaking of poetry, has lessened, as there has not been as much time free to help the students, because much of it has had to be devoted to assessing their work.

Three or four members of the English Department help by taking classes in Speech each year. The numbers in the classes vary from about seventeen to about forty, according to the groupings in other subjects. These numbers make it difficult to give all the help that is needed by individuals, but they learn a good deal from hearing one another.

The students have one period for Speech of about 50 minutes a week for about twenty-four weeks in the first year. They are helped as much as possible during this time; then members of staff put at the disposal of any students who choose to avail themselves of the opportunity, free time to help individuals.

It is difficult to assess the effect of this work on the development of the students, but I think many of them have lost a gaucheness and awkwardness and have gained a certain measure of poise and confidence, especially when they have been successful in their examination.

The work is approached with much reluctance at the beginning, because the students feel so insecure, so uncertain about how much of their own appreciation should be shown to others through their spoken work. This is particularly noticeable among first-year students, who are feeling their way with one another, and are afraid to draw attention to themselves. They are very vulnerable to the opinions of others, and they are all strangers facing a new kind of life together. It is only when they begin to feel accepted and more at home with one another, that more ease becomes apparent in their speech work, and they are willing and quite ready to take themselves less seriously and are able to be more honestly self-critical, to shed some of their inhibitions and to laugh at themselves.

When the examination time comes the majority are amazed at how they enjoy the experience, and they are genuinely pleased when they are successful, and feel it has all been worth-while. Some even say they would not mind repeating the experience.

With those who can *see* the need of all that is inculcated in the speech lessons there is no doubt that their teaching technique is bettered. They become more lively in their approach to the children and make use of all the latent possibilities in that greatest instrument for communication, their power of speech.

1c EXAMINING THE B.Ed. DEGREE (SPOKEN ENGLISH AND DRAMA)

By E. J. Burton

(Head of the Drama Department, Trent Park College of Education)

The coming of the B.Ed. degree, with Speech, Drama or "English and Drama" as one of its main components, has introduced a new situation into a pattern already sufficiently varied and perhaps bewildering to the non-specialist.

As yet, we are in the early stages of work and study for this degree. Even where the syllabus has been agreed by a particular university for colleges associated with its Institute of Education (many are still deliberating on the content and emphasis of the course, and not less on the pattern and scheme of examination) the actual and practical problems have still to be experienced. One can talk only at present in generalisations. Normally, the B.Ed. will have an education component, dealing with the theory and practise of teaching, the special stage of schooling, the philosophy of education and associated studies —psychology (child development) and sociology, for example—and alongside this *one* or *two* main fields of study, such as English or Mathematics, or (in our present consideration) Speech and Drama, or spoken English and Drama. The non-specialist must realise that such a term as B.Ed. (Drama) will have widely varying significance. It may indicate a teacher qualified in the practical skills of the study, able to work with pupils on these in school, or it may be that the possessor of this degree has only normal teacher adequacy in the arts of communication with little experience of, or interest in, the working aspects of theatre.

In most colleges the three-year teacher training course, with some additional study or tutorial work, is regarded as the first part of the degree. Students for the B.Ed. are selected *from* this general course. Hence, although at interview there may be some consideration of the intending students as potential B.Ed. candidates, this is probably strictly subordinate to the need to select primarily for the three-year teacher training course. From this, as time goes on, the B.Ed. candidate will emerge. Thus, selection is not specifically for a degree course; nor are the practical skills which may be involved in, and desirable for, an active participation in dramatic work necessarily tested. There are, of course, exceptions. Some colleges are listed, you will find, in the handbook *Training for Teaching* and equivalent reference works, as giving practical experience and training in drama and/or other arts. And in these, and in some others, there is consideration of the practical ability of the students chosen to follow such a course. But one must distinguish quite clearly between the college of education entry requirements and those of a specialist college of speech and drama, where a high standard of personal ability in the chosen art, potentially or actually, is demanded. Entry may be highly competitive because of the limited number of places and the large number of aspirants. Selection for the B.Ed. is largely—though one must not be too dogmatic for each college is an independent and flexible entity in its Institute—a matter of selection from within a general entry of "teachers in training" rather than from potential specialists.

Again, because each college has its own emphasis and established courses, one cannot dogmatise on the kind of training that may or should be given. One might hope that each college would endeavour to "round", as it were, the pattern of experience and activity which students share in the three-year course and to alert them to the implications and associated disciplines of their studies. In the case of a B.Ed. with "English and Drama" (*one* combined field of study) one would like to be assured that students have practical and first-hand experience of the expression of dramatic literature through theatre arts. But this may not necessarily be so. Equally, one would wish that where the emphasis is on practical skills, perhaps on movement or on speech, that there should be a recognition of the place of these functionally within the greater world of theatre, and the relation of that world to the community in which it exists.

Certain trends are apparent. One is the omission (after careful consideration) of the word "speech" in drawing up the syllabus in certain institutes. From the university viewpoint, "speech", it is said, would imply medical and physiological studies, and the word is thus rather ambiguous. On the other hand, B.Ed. (Drama) has been accepted by many, and it would seem quite possible that this degree will include much of the general content of the work of the "Speech and Drama" college, though somewhat wider in outlook and less demanding in personal prowess. Thus one university has arrived at the scope of its B.Ed. (Drama) degree as comprising a threefold approach:

(1) dramatic literature and its interpretation through theatre arts, actively with presentation and performance;
(2) practical skills associated with the work of each individual student, voice, movement, improvisation, actor training;
(3) the technical aspects of the study, stagecraft, costume-making and so on.

Within the various institutes, tutors interested in spoken English and Drama have fought long, and not without some success, to ensure the retention of practical work and its inclusion in some form or another in the actual assessment of the student's work for the degree. But, again, the actual scheme varies fairly widely from university to university. Further, the natural bias of the university authorities towards "academic" disciplines, as they are termed, and the traditional system of examination by written paper only have, as one would expect, been very powerful. Nonetheless, such a plan as that outlined above, with examination of the candidate's attainment and ability in various practical aspects of the work, would seem to guarantee a balanced qualification. It should create teachers not only competent to work within the English department but also to organise and maintain practical work in drama and the language arts in the school. Such a teacher, however, might not necessarily be a "speech specialist" in the commonly accepted sense, or sensitive, shall we say, to the finer shades of literary interpretation.

In short, one can only say that the significance of any B.Ed. degree depends on the particular approach of the college in which the student has trained, at least at the present moment. A glance, say, at the varying syllabuses of the colleges within the University of London Institute of Education will show some possible variations. Doubtless, as the degree is worked, there will emerge a more consistent pattern, but it is not, one feels, the policy to impose uniformity. Nor is this probably desirable. One can only advise those interested to study the syllabus of any particular college. The three-years course, however modified, is at present the general study from which the B.Ed. for that college emerges. There is over the country possibly one main dividing line: that between those offering English and Drama, or "spoken English" with English, and those specifically claiming to follow "Drama" with its implications of practical work leading to theatre.

It may be surmised that the first group will tend rather to study general communication, the development of spoken English skills in class, the concept of "oracy" and the appreciation of communication from others, in literature, poetry and drama, within this general concept of "communication". But, here again, any one college may demur. The most positive information will be derived from the actual statements and syllabus of each institution.

There is, of course, one great advantage in the B.Ed. in any field. It is, or should be, closely linked with practical teaching. Anyone who possesses it must prove to be a successful teacher in classroom conditions. Moreover, there is a new stress on linking the main field of study *with* practical teaching. Credit will be given for this, and deep consideration devoted to teaching within the special field. Thus it can be assumed that B.Ed. (Drama) will imply successful teaching of the subject in the school, though it may well be mainly through the associated educational activities rather than actual "play production", for better, for worse; and that a B.Ed. with "English and spoken English" will signify a potential teacher who can communicate adequately with his pupils, and guide the children themselves, to engage fruitfully in various patterns of spoken communication and artistic expression. But it could also be that the potential teacher has been mainly concerned with "linguistics" rather than with the work of a "teacher of voice and speech". He may lack the gifts traditionally associated with the speech specialist.

The universities will, it seems, to judge from the lead given by some, rightly insist that the B.Ed. candidate should be carefully assessed during teaching practice in his three-year course for proficiency in his chosen field *as a teacher*. Normally some time roughly half-way through his three-year course he will be seen as potential "B.Ed. material". Further tutorials and assignments will be given to him; and at this stage one must hope that (as now demanded by two universities) his teaching in his chosen field will be seen by specialists. The ability to communicate with his pupils, to share and to encourage the various activities of speech, his own adequacy in voice, manner and sensitivity of expression should be noted and fostered in the actual classroom. Later, in actual "examination", he may be required to state and justify his approach to particular tasks or school activities; such statement in a *viva* should be not merely for content, but also to assess (with due consideration of the unnatural strain often imposed by such an examination) his own powers of selection, arrangement and clarity of expression. Whatever may be said theoretically about the difficulty of this and the drawback for the nervous student, long experience of hearing students on teaching practice, and examining them by *viva*, encourages me to say that the satisfactory can be separated quite conclusively from the unsatisfactory, the insensitive and uncommunicating from the sensitive and aware. "Relationship" between the speaker and the listener, whether class or tutor, is usually fairly clear, and should be carefully watched during the period of training. It is in this "period of training" that observation and assessment should be made. I do not think that the artificial lesson, put on specially for an examination, or the use of the tape-recorder to attempt an analysis of students' voices, will avail much. These matters must be attended to during the three years *previous* to the final and definitive B.Ed. year. *It is speech in the natural group situation which counts.*

It may well be that amongst graduates from the colleges listed in *Training for Teaching* as giving special attention to drama or to spoken English the standard of attainment in speech and drama will be high. But the emphasis of the B.Ed. is not on such individual attainment. The possession of the degree should, however, mean that the teacher is capable of sensitive encouragement of the work of his pupils; that he, or she, can "move" and appreciate good movement; that he or she can speak with assurance and clarity. As an examiner one would expect the candidate to have good vocal quality, an engaging manner and an ability to develop these qualities creatively in his pupils. The candidate should show vitality and imagination in his approach to all dramatic work and be capable of making literature live through his active response to situation, event and character. It is outside the scope or space of this article to outline methods and approaches that students might be expected to exemplify. They are not different from those implied in other sections of this book.

Finally—and this is important—in no sense will the coming of

B.Ed. (spoken English) or B. Ed.(Drama) usurp the field of work of the "specialist" teacher of speech and drama from the "specialist" college. In these there is an emphasis on practical skills, the actual "doing" and continued progressive quality of attainment by the pupil, which should supplement the more general work of the teacher possessing the B.Ed. It may well be, of course, that a student obtains qualifications in both these aspects. But if I were a headmaster I should look to my "B.Ed." teacher to organise and correlate the English work alongside his colleagues, with particular reference to spoken English or drama, as the case might be. To secure the fullest appreciation of spoken poetry, to present that often maligned activity, "the school play", to stimulate real creativity in classroom drama and the specialised form of dance, mime and movement; I should still engage a specialist teacher from one of the colleges of speech and drama recognised by the Department of Education. I might, of course, find that my "B.Ed." teacher experienced in general linguistic skills, understanding the needs of pupils, able to promote discussion and debate, well furnished with ideas and sensitive himself in communication, might also be capable of taking over play production and have skills in the interpretative arts.

Although the two qualifications may seem to cover the same ground there is a difference in emphasis. We must be aware of this difference.

What has been said relates in the main to the B.Ed. degree as it is gradually emerging in the English universities; in Scotland, where the pattern of teacher training is somewhat different, the new B.Ed. will necessarily incorporate such distinctive features as mark the Scottish educational system and emphasis. A further source of confusion (for the headmaster or education officer examining the credentials of candidates for a post) is the existence already of certain degrees in education which are pedagogical and academic in content and which do not necessarily imply the expertise of their holder as a *practical teacher*. There are, however, two further considerations to be noted, especially by any person or body responsible for appointments: in some universities it will be possible for candidates to take not only, for example, B.Ed. with "Drama" but also B.Ed. with the "teaching of Speech and Drama", i.e. the whole of their special field of study is concerned with teaching methods and materials. Such a candidate must be regarded as very probably suitable for a specialist post, though, again, there is no necessary implication that he or she is particularly proficient or talented in the art which he or she is concerned to teach. And last, but not least, any person possessing a B.Ed. degree may, when qualifying as a teacher, have specialised in primary education and its teaching tasks. In all this, of course, the writer seeks merely to indicate various possibilities to be taken into consideration by anyone attempting to establish qualifications; there is no reflection upon or criticism of these. His own firm faith is, however, and that is supported by the author of this book, herself an examiner for B.Ed. spoken English and Drama, that the B.Ed. must indicate real and practical skill as a teacher, whatever the area and emphasis of the special field of study.

1d B.Ed. COURSE IN SPOKEN ENGLISH AND DRAMA AT ABERDEEN
By Elizabeth Henry

The B.Ed. students in Aberdeen have a completely different programme from the diploma students from the beginning of their course. They are required to take at least five subjects, at least one of which must be selected from Arts and Crafts, spoken English and Drama, Music or Physical Education. The time allocation is officially 200 hours, but there is an understanding that no student should be required to attend for more than 150 hours in a session.

The practical subjects are all preceded by a 100-hour introductory course, since no previous knowledge or ability can be presupposed in these.

The course in spoken English and Drama has been deliberately left flexible, with as much scope for personal choice as possible. All students must give evidence of reasonable competence on a stage. More importance, however, is attached to their ability to mount small classroom productions. Similarly, each student takes two oral tests, discussing aspects of the work in which he has specialised. But he is also seen at work in the classroom, and his ability to promote good speaking and active listening is gauged in these conditions.

Students each choose an area of special study. This again involves gaining practical experience rather than theoretical knowledge, and many enthusiasms have been fostered in the past two years.

There is an active team who have chosen to specialise in spoken English in school, and some of these have developed particular interests such as language development from birth to infant school years; a survey of the uses of the interview situation; a survey of the uses of the tape-recorder in the primary school, and so on.

One student who has specialised in tape-recording has made a study of modern methods of teaching French in school; another of modern methods of teaching history.

Others have made Children's Theatre their special activity, and are beginning to specialise in aspects of creative drama.

Closed-circuit television and film-making groups have been formed, but these courses were at first hampered by inadequate equipment. This has been remedied, and the closed-circuit television group are learning how to present simple pieces of instruction in visual terms; while a film-making team is making a visual record of aspects of the course.

This is fundamentally a practical course, and it is accepted that students who have had no previous experience of this work cannot in the short space of a session become talented actors. Nor can they profess a knowledge in depth of dramatic history or the theatrical crafts.

But they can become imaginative teachers of spoken English, which includes classroom drama.

They can develop an awareness of the conditions which are essential to the promotion of lively speaking and listening situations in the classroom. They are not necessarily performers in themselves, nor is it particularly their duty to promote performance from their pupils.

But by creating the right climate and conditions for a wide variety of speaking and listening activities, they will be making an invaluable contribution to the total development of their pupils; for improved language ability has repercussions in every aspect of the pupil's life. In learning to express himself happily and confidently he develops, not only academically, but socially, emotionally and spiritually as well.

From their written work, it is obvious that amongst these twenty-seven students in the first B.Ed. degree course there are some who are fully aware of the exciting possibilities of this stimulating new field; students whose enthusiasm has steadily mounted throughout the course.

The theses which they are producing in their project work, many of them illustrated with tapes, promise to be of real value, making a positive contribution to the wider experimental work of the department.

Some of these students will find it impossible to abandon their allegiance to spoken English during the remainder of their course, although as yet there is no provision for an advanced course in a practical subject.

When such a course develops, even more exciting new possibilities will appear. But they will only develop to the full if we keep our courses flexible enough to allow the student to follow his real interests and enthusiasms.

In such an unexplored territory, it is surely folly to cling to old-established ways because they feel safer. It is equally unwise to abandon everything that has previously been accepted as the normal work of spoken English.

But by promoting the spirit of experiment, giving students all guidance and encouragement to work actively in their chosen fields, we open ourselves to the limitless possibilities and fascinating diversity of spoken English, or Oracy, which Wilkinson has so well described as "not a subject, but a condition of learning in all subjects".*

2. THE EXAMINING OF FOREIGN STUDENTS IN SPOKEN ENGLISH

By Basil Harvey

(Director of Examinations of Foreign Students for the English Speaking Board)

"Can You Speak English?"

It is literally true that millions of foreigners learn English, but for most of them the emphasis is on the reading and writing of the

* Wilkinson, *Spoken English*, Birmingham University.

language. Speech is treated as less important. Though some instruction in pronunciation is always given, the teaching is often—inevitably—in the hands of those who are more at home with the text of "Macbeth" than with everyday conversational usage. There are plenty of examinations for foreigners, but very few indeed that have an oral test of any practical value. The English Speaking Board is, as far as we know, the only body that examines in English speech, and nothing else. By concentrating on the oral side we have acquired exceptional experience in this sphere.

(i) English as a World Language

English is the first of the world languages. Not only is it remarkable for the number of its native speakers, who were estimated some years ago at 250 millions, but also it is the most widely accepted of second languages. It is unique in its spread and prestige, being the language of some of the most powerful and progressive communities in the world, spoken in every quarter of the globe. Moreover, its virtues as a language are also outstanding, as it has a relatively simple grammatical structure and a remarkably rich vocabulary that is well adapted to everyday use, and to scientific and commercial purposes, as well as to more literary uses. The wealth of its literature means that the foreign student has, as he progresses, the entrée to the rich treasury of our written works, from Shakespeare to Graham Greene.

So our native language is something in which we are entitled to take pride. As our status as a world power lessens and our imperial responsibilities dwindle, we can comfort ourselves with the thought that English as a world language is second to none. It follows that we should hold our mother tongue in the greatest respect, and that in speaking it—and, of course, in writing it—we should set ourselves standards worthy of its greatness.

(ii) The Teaching of English to Foreigners

Such standards should be applied to the teaching of the language to those for whom it is a foreign language. There is no lack of opportunity for teaching it. Not only are there many here, whether English men and women or from abroad, whose function will be to teach English all over the world, but there are also thousands who come here for short "holiday" courses, for prolonged periods of professional study, or with the intention of settling in our country either as doctors, nurses, etc., or as industrial workers. For all these, in differing degrees, a high standard of spoken English is essential.

There is much admirable teaching now given to such visitors or immigrants. In recent years the techniques of teaching English to foreigners have been greatly developed. There are excellent courses of a practical kind, and a wide variety of textbooks for study. "Language schools", which vary greatly in efficiency but the best of which are first-rate, have proliferated in the metropolis and the more favoured sea-side resorts. It is a pity that some of these schools are worth little, and that teachers in them have no specialised training. This means that a good deal of ineffective or irrelevant teaching still goes on. Sometimes literature of the past, with little relevance to the speech of today, is studied in an unimaginative way; sometimes the grammar—and then in an outmoded form—is made the basis of the teaching; and when the spoken language is given its due importance, it is sometimes taught with the wrong emphasis, such as insistence on the "purity" of vowel sounds of the R.P. kind.

All these visitors can, and many of them do, benefit from a course of graded exams in spoken English, if the criteria for such exams are the right ones, and their structure is such as to cater for the whole gamut of students. These may be children of 12 or so from a European country, who have learnt English at school for two or three years, and who are having a holiday-with-study over here; they may be adult industrial workers from India or Pakistan who have never previously learnt a word of English; they may be young students for whom English has been only a second or even third language for study; they may be advanced students who have read and spoken English for many years.

(iii) E.S.B. Exams for Foreign Students

The examinations for foreign students conducted by the English Speaking Board aim to cater for all these levels. When they were first conceived about twelve years ago, three grades were provided; the increasing number of candidates—which indicates the demand for some sort of qualification in speech—has caused the Board to extend the number of grades to seven. The lowest, which asks for mutual intelligibility on a very simple level, is within the range of a child who has learnt English at school in his own country for two or three years and who has probably spent a month with an English family. The highest asks for a pretty thorough mastery of our spoken tongue, with some background of literary study and a sound grasp of English phonetics.

In general, the exams are designed to encourage the development of ease and proficiency in the everyday use of spoken English, and the main criterion can be defined as mutual intelligibility on increasingly higher levels.

As the grades progress step by step from the lowest level, the syllabus demands greater accuracy in the use of English sounds, stressing and speech tunes or intonation patterns. It forges the essential link with reading and writing, by such means as asking for the reading aloud of a piece of dialogue (e.g. about a shopping expedition) that the candidate has written, a reading from a newspaper or book he has read, or the giving of a short talk with the aid of notes that he has previously made. In the highest grades some literary study is more closely associated with the exam, all teachers and examiners of English being well aware that the spoken tongue is inseparable from literature, which enriches it in range of vocabulary and nuance of expression.

(iv) Preparation for E.S.B. Exams; Aspects of English Speech

The sort of preparation needed for the exams can be deduced from the above, but the various facets can usefully be set out in greater detail.

Sounds. In general, vowel sounds cause more difficulty than consonants, because of our numerous diphthongs. But some consonants or consonantal combinations may be a source of trouble. The two *th* sounds, the aspirate, and the *r* sound are obvious examples.

Intonations. Speech which disregards the variety of speech tunes which every language possesses, is never live speech. The characteristic intonations for questions, exclamations, etc., can be learnt, and imitated, at an early stage. Where the background teaching has been primarily concerned with the written word and silent reading for comprehension, a candidate's reading will sometimes reveal his unawareness of this aspect of speech. Or he will often, having grasped the pattern of a common intonation like the falling pitch at the end of a statement, repeat the pattern mechanically without much reference to the meaning.

Stressing. Pity any poor foreigner who has to cope with the vagaries of our syllable stressing! Not only is it impossible to give rules of practical help in deciding which syllable to stress (*de'monstrate* but *remonstr'ate*; *host'ile* but *hostil'ity*, etc.), but also English usage is variable, and becoming more so (*contr'oversy* or *contro'versy*, *ex'quisite* or *exquis'ite*, *research'* or *re'search*, etc.). Though these controversial pronunciations are matters that arouse our prejudices and raise our blood-pressure, they are fortunately of no vital concern to the foreigner. The proper stressing—where we all agree upon it—is something that he will—perhaps—learn from experience, through constant listening to good models either in personal relationships or in the language laboratory.

Grammar. The basic grammar is simple enough, but two aspects often cause trouble. Our strong verbs, which change the vowel in the past tense, and sometimes again in the past participle (*hang, hung, hung*; *sing, sang, sung*; *see, saw, seen*), and the more wildly irregular (*go, went, gone*), are important for acceptable English speech. Fortunately they have often been learnt mechanically, like the Latin declensions and conjugations hammered into the older generation, very early in the study of English. The other chief source of grammatical uncertainty is probably to be found in our auxiliary verbs (*am, will, can, may, must*, etc.) which are admittedly confusing. We have to remember that though constant usage since we began to speak has made us at home (more or less) with a set of subtle distinctions, the stranger to our language has to master something much harder than mere vocabulary, and learn, as indeed we ourselves have to do, the particular "register" in which a word or phrase has a particular application or shade of meaning.

Idiomatic usage. This is distinguished in English by its wide variety, its nuances of meaning or emotive colouring, and its duplication of forms (e.g. *face* and *face up to*), and is perhaps the knottiest of the learner's problems. But he can, and should, be introduced quite early to a number of colloquial idioms, the more literary ones being unconsciously absorbed as he widens his reading. Slang may present a problem here. It should not be ruled out; but phrases like "O.K." and "Yep" (for "yes") are objectionable because they suggest a lack of courtesy in the particular speech situation of an exam. The overuse of "fillers" (or "fill-in" words and phrases) like "sort of", "I mean" and the ubiquitous "you know", are also undesirable; but we have to recognise that they have been picked up in live speech contact with our countrymen—a better way of acquiring colloquial idiom than learning lists from a book.

Spelling. In dealing with foreigners, our only possible posture is an apologetic one. Our spelling is, of course, wildly illogical and eccentric. We must be tolerant of mispronunciations based on merely reading our language; but should expect the commoner oddities (no *l* sound in "should", no *gh* sound in "might", etc., *ad lib*) to have been confronted and mastered.

The neutral vowel. All unaccented vowels except short *i* (as in "credit") and short *e* (as in "belong") usually have a sound that is approximately "er" (ə). These neutral vowels are an essential feature of easy, natural English speech. At a time when an increasing number of speakers on radio and television are apparently unaware of this, so that "the Minister" becomes "thee (ði:) Minister", instead of "ther (ðə) Minister", and "a book" is pronounced "ay (ei) book" instead of "er (ə) book", we hope that foreigners are early taught its proper use, and not encouraged in this misguided attempt at "correctness" which reveals the speaker as sadly inorate.

Interpretation. Reading aloud means interpretation, in vocal terms, of what is read. The speaker has to understand the writer's words, and to convey both the intellectual content and the emotive colouring. This is a difficult exercise, of which many educated Englishmen are hardly capable. Therefore we cannot expect very much of those to whom our language is a foreign one. But we would be right to demand, at any rate in the higher grades, some sensitivity to both kinds of meaning. A misplaced pause or emphasis may indicate a misunderstanding of the sense of a sentence; a failure to respond to,

9

for instance, a passage of exciting narrative by quickening the tempo, etc., implies a lack of sensitivity to the mood of what is read.

Perfection? We all know of people who are alleged to speak a foreign tongue "exactly like a native". Our kindly compatriots sometimes assure foreigners that, by their speech, they "could be taken for English". We may view such judgements with scepticism. This kind of standard, a total identification with all the nuances of a foreign tongue, must be very, very rarely achieved. Should we demand it in a final exam of a graded series? I think not; first, because it is almost impossible of achievement; next, because this total identification hardly seems a worth-while object—except possibly in the training of spies; and finally because a slight colouring of "foreignness" is attractive rather than not, and incidentally will often result in the speaker's receiving a broader tolerance, vocally speaking, than we would allow to our fellow-countrymen.

(v) Examining Methods and Techniques

An exam of foreign students may be of the "group" kind that is advocated by the E.S.B. and has been their standard practice for years. But it is not necessarily the right form for foreign students, whose one overriding aim is mastery of the spoken language. In the main the "interview" type of exam is better suited to one struggling to speak in a medium that is not a natural one to him; and though he may readily undergo a group exam with a few others who have worked with him and form a harmonious band of brothers, or in the presence of a few sympathetic English listeners, the "interview" situation is that in general use by E.S.B. examiners.

The examiner will take pains to make the right relationship with the candidate. Though, especially as an "interviewer", he is in a position of authority, he will alleviate the weight of his inquisitorial function by a friendly and informal approach to the business in hand. To put the candidates at ease is essential for good results, and when they are obviously nervous, he will be prepared to spend a little valuable time in casual chat in order to ease tensions, before he begins to assess their proficiency.

As in all oral exams, the examiner himself will have to do a good deal of talking. At the beginning this is desirable for two reasons:

putting the candidates at ease, as mentioned above, and getting them used to his voice. With foreign students, in the lower grades, he will take pains to speak very clearly and rather more slowly than usual, though he need never adopt an over-articulated form of speech. After that he will be careful not to talk too much. He must frame his questions in such a way that they cannot be disposed of by a mere "yes" or "no". They will be, wherever possible, open-ended, encouraging full answers. He must resist the tendency some of us have to *teach* the candidate, though he will occasionally have to correct a flagrant mispronunciation or the obvious misuse of some key word. As a general rule, the candidates should do more talking than the examiner; the higher the grade, the higher the proportion of their contribution.

In every kind of exam, written or spoken, the main problem of assessment lies in the middle range. An experienced examiner will very soon make up his mind about the particularly good or the abysmally bad. It is those of moderate proficiency who will give him most trouble. He may have to extend the conversation or the reading, to ask easy or probing questions, and to suspend his final judgement until he has met other candidates. This is especially so if there is a certificate at stake.

Where a number of examiners are dealing with hundreds of candidates, it is desirable to hold a "co-ordinating exam" at the beginning of the operation. Several candidates of different grades, chosen where possible from those who have already taken a spoken English exam, are provided. The examiners present take turns in examining the candidates, preferably with two of them, one more and one less experienced, working in partnership. The others, sitting in the background, make their own assessment, and after each candidate all the assessments are compared and discussed. After a session of this sort they can feel that they have a good grasp of the standards required.

The aim of these exams is to measure proficiency in speaking English, and the syllabus sets out in some detail the requirements, grade by grade. This is not the place to discuss considerations, which apply to all exams, of validity and reliability. It is sufficient to remark that these two conceptions, however satisfactorily achieved, do not in themselves make a good exam. It is more important that the exam should exert a salutary influence on the teaching that preceded it, and should prove a practical stimulus to a wider and more effective use of our language.

Examiners find the work demanding, even exhausting, but never boring. They are meeting a succession of *people*, receiving the impact of varied personalities, and adapting their approach to each one. This demands an open mind, much tolerance and as much sensitivity as can be mustered. Their rewards are their successes in drawing out the nervous or reticent; their delight in lively and intelligent reactions when they are met with; and the light relief that smoothes their way when some misuse of our tongue provides a flash of unintended humour.

Let me conclude with a few examples of minor mishandlings of words that have occurred in E.S.B. exams to the delight of the examiner and to the mitigation of his ardours. A French boy of 16 explained how he met an English girl, but found her uncongenial, saying, "She was not my tea-cup". A young man, speaking of the English family he was staying with, surprised his examiner, a lady, by telling her that every day after lunch "he sported with his hostess for an hour". She was relieved to learn that he was receiving instruction in the mysteries of cricket. And there was the young lady who, talking to the examiner of the amenities she had met at our sea-side resorts, told him that there were many beautiful beaches at the seaside. But though she had been at pains to acquire the English short *i* sound, as in "sit", which does not occur in her native French, she did not clearly grasp its use in English, and gave the word "beaches" a short *i* sound, presenting the examiner with an unexpected image of the holiday scene.

3. SUGGESTED PLAN FOR ASSESSING SPOKEN ENGLISH ON A WIDE SCALE IN ANY ADMINISTRATIVE AREA

By Elizabeth Henry

Assessment can only be meaningful when there is a total structure of progressive assessment from primary school until the end of the pupil's school career, and when this is related to a national standard.

Assessment should be broadly based, covering the various areas of spoken work engaged in in the classroom, and would be in the nature of a profile of the pupil's progress in speech.

It follows that within each school year there would be a running assessment, and that the obvious person to conduct this would be the class teacher.

The most economical way of initiating this would seem to be as follows:

(a) The appointment by the headmaster in each school of a teacher or teachers with a special interest in this work to organise the assessment arrangements within the school.

(b) The setting up of a local working party which would include members of the city, borough or county speech (or speech and drama) department and of the college of education speech department, together with the teacher-representatives of each school.

(c) Subdividing the above group into sections with common problems, e.g. upper secondary, lower secondary and junior. There would probably be a remedial section, and other sub-divisions might suggest themselves later. (This is only a suggested subdivision. Some areas might prefer a cross-section in each group.)

Regular meetings would be required to introduce teachers to methods of assessment and to establish some sort of shared philosophy in approaching this work.

The English Speaking Board system of a four-part test with a five-point grading scale has proved to be not only workable but stimu-lating, and there seems little point in seeking less well-tried alterna-tives.

The annual visit from an external examiner is necessary from the point of view of standardising marks. It is also invaluable as a demonstration of methods, not only of assessing, but also of *teaching* spoken English.

It might conceivably be of even greater value if the examiner were to pay two shorter visits to each school. The first, half-way through the year, could establish a relationship with the pupils, and would be primarily for the poetry/prose/drama/reading aloud part of the test. The second would be geared to the pupil's personal projects: assessing their ability to inform, explain and instruct.

The pupils selected for the external examiner's visit would probably be a selection of those who would be due to leave that section of the school at the end of the session.

An agreed fee would be paid to the English Speaking Board per examiner day. Once a school's examiner time allocation had been arrived at, it would be possible to estimate the exact expense involved, in that it would be up to the school to present only the number of pupils that could be examined in the available time.

The external examiners would receive a fee from the English Speaking Board for their services, and would be mainly local. Expenses would be met by the local authority. A co-ordinating meeting would be held annually during the visit of the Director of the English Speaking Board.

The examiners would be drawn from the speech staffs of the city, borough or county education department and of the college of education. Members of speech departments in other nearby areas would be invited from time to time to exchange ideas and co-ordinate standards.

Questions and Statements for Discussion in Colleges of Education and at In-service Teachers' Courses

1. Boy in a grammar school sixth form (incapable of translating print into the rhythm of spoken English): "I haven't read aloud in class for five years." Discuss this.

2. "They don't talk in *my* lesson." A complacent remark overheard in a secondary school staff room.

3. All experience demands the response of the senses through *movement*. Mental development must be connected with movement and be dependent on it. How much of the curriculum is really informed with this idea? How can we incorporate it into the spoken English assessment?

4. Movement—and of course speech is movement—has great importance in mental development provided that the action is connected with the mental activity. Limiting muscular activity to silent reading and writing not only cramps the individual physically but cramps his development as a social being.

5. The child who has a "head" (and heart!) start in life is the one who has been talked to and listened to by kindly, intelligent adults in the early years. How can we in schools supply this omission in detailed practical ways?

6. We learn to speak by speaking, but we can only speak with vitality and interest if our experiences are rich. But a child may have rich experiences and not realise it because he is short of *producible language*. Only if he has heard language used richly from human beings who have heightened awareness about their own experiences and those of others can he acquire the ability to share his own. What are we doing in the colleges of education to equip teachers for this supremely important function?

7. In his book *Language and Education* F. D. Flower writes: "If this society is to be democratic its members must be able to speak to each other with understanding. . . ." How much time in school is spent on thoughtful, fruitful, critical conversation and discussion?

8. Are our examinations too much concerned with the short-term memorising of facts (teaching) rather than assessment of independent action and discovery (learning)? How can a widely based spoken English assessment give scope and stimulus to this kind of learning?

9. "Education is a preparation for life." Appraise and criticise this well-worn platitude. Children are living *now*.

10. In her book *Education Through Experience in the Infant School Years* Edna Mellor says:

> As the child goes about his work, climbing, building, constructing, pretending, experimenting and tidying he will make use of these new words in the running commentary that so often accompanies absorbing work of any kind, and so they will become part of his vocabulary and his speech will be enriched.

In secondary schools, if we continued with the same kind of active learning on individual lines, could not each child benefit factually and linguistically from *oral* expositions presented in an orderly way by himself and his colleagues? Could not, in fact, the spoken English or "communications" test be a good end product in interdisciplinary enquiry?

11. How can we, in planning a spoken English test and in the preparation towards it, avoid the possibility of giving the less academic child another situation in which he may fail? In other words how can we make it his own *personal* test?

12. Are we in danger in prescribing a spoken English test of inhibiting or penalising racy idiomatic talk which may be much richer and more evocative than the pedants' well-structured language? Give your own examples from your teaching or teaching practice which show unorthodox but vivid communication. Then ask yourself: What kind of speech do you want for your *own* child?

13. "Perception takes time," said Margaret Macmillan. How would you ensure that poetry, drama, music and art classes really involve the senses fully and critically? Is it not necessary to know a few things really "by heart" (i.e. with the senses and muscles involved) before we can fully appreciate them?

Should this heightened perception—the response to language and experience richer than our own—not be part of the spoken English test?

14. In the *School and the Child* John Dewey said: "An end which is the child's own carries him on to possess the means of its accomplishment." Discuss this in relation to the *oral* sharing of his accomplishments. Should not this happen at each stage in school life so that the child and his accomplishments are strengthened by the appreciation and criticism of others?

References and Background Reading

E.S.B. Pamphlets and Articles

What is Spoken English? Can it be Examined in General Education?: CHRISTABEL
BURNISTON (1962).
Spoken English Examined. Widening Horizons: ELIZABETH HENRY (1964).
Concord through the Spoken Word: CHRISTABEL BURNISTON (1964).
English Speech, Vols. 1–13 (1954–67).
Plato to Plowden, article by CHRISTABEL BURNISTON. *English Speech*, Vol. 12.

*H.M.S.O. Pamphlets and Publications containing Guidance on Oral
Teaching and Examining*

Teaching and Examining.
Reading in the Primary School (Edinburgh, 1954).
Composition in the Primary School (Edinburgh, 1957).
Half our Future. Newsom Report (1963).
Examinations Bulletins. Schools Council 1–12.
English. Working Paper No. 3. Schools Council (1965).
Examinations Bulletin No. 5. *School-based Examinations* (1965).
Examinations Bulletin No. 11. *C.S.E. Trial Examinations—Oral English* (1966).
The Plowden Report on Primary Education (1967).
Society and the Young School Leaver: Working Paper No. 11. Schools Council (1967).

N.A.T.E. Bulletins

Criteria of Success in English.
C.S.E. English—an interim report. Autumn 1964.
Some Aspects of Oracy. Summer 1965.
Poetry. Spring 1966.
Primary English. Autumn 1966.
English Examined. A Survey of "O" level papers (1966).

Publications of the Curriculum Laboratory, University of London, Goldsmiths' College

Ideas—a monthly bulletin on the concept of the IDE-based curriculum.
* The role of the school in a changing society: First pilot course for experienced teachers (1965).
* The raising of the school-leaving age: Second pilot course for experienced teachers (1965).
* The education of the socially handicapped: Third pilot course for experienced teachers (1966).
* 14–18: The education of the young school leaver: Fourth pilot course for experienced teachers (1966).
* Fifth pilot course (1967).

Principles of English Teaching

English for the English: GEORGE SAMPSON (1921).
Teaching English through Self Expression: E. J. BURTON (Evans, 1939).
Education and the University: F. R. LEAVIS (Chatto & Windus, 1943).
Purpose in the Curriculum: STANLEY NISBET (University of London Press, 1957).
English for Maturity: DAVID HOLBROOK (Cambridge University Press, 1961).
The Vital Approach: D. MATTAM (Pergamon Press, 1963).
The Use of Imagination: WILLIAM WALSH (Chatto & Windus, 1959).
Sense and Sensitivity: J. W. P. CREBER (University of London Press, 1965).
Topics in English: G. SUMMERFIELD (Batsford, 1965).
Who Teaches English? PROFESSOR BORIS FORD (N.A.T.E. Bulletin II, 1965).
Good Enough for the Children? JOHN BLACKIE (Faber & Faber, 1963).
Language in Education: F. D. FLOWER (Longmans, Green, 1966).
The Right Response: SYDNEY BOLT (Hutchinson, 1966).
The Disappearing Dais: FRANK WHITEHEAD (Chatto & Windus, 1966).

Language and Linguistics

Language in Society: PROFESSOR M. M. LEWIS (Nelson, 1947).
The Use of English: RANDOLPH QUIRK (Longmans, Green, 1962).
Language, Thought and Personality in Infancy and Childhood: PROFESSOR M. M. LEWIS (Harrap, 1963).
The Tongues of Men and of Speech: J. R. FIRTH (Oxford University Press, 1964).
Social Structure. Language and Learning Education Research, Vol. III.

* Obtainable on request, 5s. each.

General Educational Philosophy and Practice with reference to growth of language

The Nursery School: MARGARET MACMILLAN (J. M. Dent, Revised ed. 1930).
The Ethical End in Education: MARGARET MACMILLAN (out of print).
The Absorbent Mind: MARIE MONTESSORI (Theosophical Publishing House, 5th ed., 1964).
The School and the Child: JOHN DEWEY (University of Chicago Press).
Education through Experience in the Infant School Years: EDNA MELLOR (Basil Blackwell, 1950).
An Experiment in Education: SYBIL MARSHALL (Cambridge University Press, 1963).
A Question of Living: R. F. MACKENZIE (Collins, 1963).
Total Education: M. L. JACKS (Kegan Paul French, 1947).
Thresholds of Literacy: ALAN D. PULLEN—English in Education No. 1, Vol. I (N.A.T.E., 1967).
The Place of English in Interdisciplinary Enquiry—English in Education No. 1, Vol. I (N.A.T.E., 1967).

Spoken English

Speech and Communication in the Primary School: CLIVE SANSOM (A. & C. Black, 1965).
Speak for Yourself: AUDREY and DAVID PRICE (Allman, 1965).
Speech for Life: CHRISTABEL BURNISTON (Pergamon Press, 1965).
Speak for Yourselves: CASCIANI (Harrap, 1966).
Spoken English in Further Education: CHRISTABEL BURNISTON (Methuen, 1966).
Spoken English for C.S.E.: ARTHUR WISE (Harrap, 1966).
Spoken English: ANDREW WILKINSON (University Education Department, Birmingham).
On Speaking Terms: KEITH DADDS (E. J. Arnold, 1966).
Speech Education: two monographs: GRACE LAYMAN and ALISTAIR RIACH (Faculty of Education, Memorial University of Newfoundland).
The Scope of Oracy: BASIL HARVEY (Pergamon Press, 1968).

Drama in Education

Drama in Schools: E. J. BURTON (Herbert Jenkins, 1955).
Leap to Life: ALAN GARRARD and JOHN WILES (Chatto & Windus, 1957).
An introduction to Child Drama (shortened form of *Child Drama*): PETER SLADE (University of London Press, 1958).
Improvisation in Drama: JOHN HODGSON and ERNEST RICHARDS (Methuen, 1966).
Please Miss, Can I play God?: JOAN HAGGERTY (Methuen, 1966).
Development through Drama: BRIAN WAY (Longmans, Green, 1966).

Speaking and Appreciation of Poetry

The Adventure of Poetry: FRANK KENDON (A. & C. Black, 1932).
The Appreciation of Poetry: P. GURREY (Oxford University Press, 1935).
Poetry for You: CECIL DAY LEWIS (Basil Blackwell, 1944).
Introductions to Part I and Part II. *Anthology of Spoken Verse and Prose:* CHRISTABEL
    BURNISTON (Oxford University Press, 1957).
Speaking Poetry: GEOFFREY CRUMP (Methuen, 1953; republished Dobson, 1964).
Teaching Poetry: JAMES REEVES (Heinemann, 1958).
Imperfect Speakers: BETTY MULCAHY (Poetry Review, 1964).
To Speak True: BETTY MULCAHY (Pergamon Press (in preparation)).

Practical Books on Voice and Speech

Vital Speech: HAROLD RIPPER (Methuen, 1938).
Speech and Drama: ROSE BRUFORD (Methuen, 1948).
Good Speech in the Making: MUSGRAVE HORNER (Rigby, 1959).
Voice Production and Speech: GRETA COLSON (Museum Press, 1963).
Verbal Dynamics: JOCELYN BELL & CHRISTABEL BURNISTON (in preparation).

Oral Examining

English in the Certificate of Secondary Education (Cambridge University Press, 1964).
The Sedgley Park Experiment (an article in *Semper Fidelis*, college magazine, 1965).
Examinations Bulletin No. 11. *C.S.E. Trial Examinations—Oral English* (H.M.S.O.,
    1966).
Examining Oral English in Schools: P. J. HITCHMAN (Methuen, 1966).
An examination that makes sense: ELIZABETH HENRY (an article in *Education in
    the North*, 1966).
Developments in the testing of spoken English within the State School Educational
    System: BARBARA CLAYPOLE (article in *Speech & Drama*, Autumn, 1966,
    Journal of the Society of Teachers of Speech and Drama).

Handbooks and Syllabuses of the C.S.E. Regional Boards

ASSOCIATED LANCASHIRE SCHOOLS EXAMINING BOARD, 77 Whitworth Street,
    Manchester, 1.
EAST ANGLIAN REGIONAL EXAMINATIONS BOARD, The Lindens, Lexden Road,
    Colchester.
EAST MIDLAND REGIONAL EXAMINATIONS BOARD, Robins Wood House, Robins
    Wood Road, Aspley, Nottingham.
METROPOLITAN REGIONAL EXAMINATIONS BOARD, 23–24 Henrietta Street, London,
    W.C. 2
MIDDLESEX REGIONAL EXAMINING BOARD, Education Offices, High Street,
    Wealdstone, Harrow.
NORTH REGIONAL EXAMINATIONS BOARD, Neville Hall, Westgate Road,
    Newcastle-upon-Tyne, 1.

NORTH WESTERN SECONDARY SCHOOL EXAMINATIONS BOARD, 54 Whitworth Street, Manchester, 1.

SOUTHERN REGIONAL EXAMINATIONS BOARD, 53 London Road, Southampton.

SOUTH-EAST REGIONAL EXAMINATIONS BOARD, 2 & 4 Mount Ephraim Road, Tunbridge Wells.

SOUTH WESTERN REGIONAL EXAMINATIONS BOARD, 23–29 Marsh Street, Bristol, 1.

WELSH JOINT EDUCATION COMMITTEE, 30 Cathedral Road, Cardiff.

WEST MIDLANDS EXAMINATIONS BOARD, Norfolk House, Smallbrook Ringway, Birmingham, 5.

WEST YORKSHIRE AND LINDSEY REGIONAL EXAMINING BOARD, 136 Derbyshire Lane, Sheffield, 8.

YORKSHIRE REGIONAL EXAMINATIONS BOARD, 7–9 Cambridge Road, Harrogate, Yorkshire.